Workshops

Workshops

Designing

and

Facilitating

Experiential

Learning

Jeff E. Brooks-Harris
Susan R. Stock-Ward

SAGE Publications
International Educational and Professional Publisher
Thousand Oaks   London   New Delhi

For information:

SAGE Publications, Inc.
2455 Teller Road
Thousand Oaks, California 91320
E-mail: order@sagepub.com

SAGE Publications Ltd.
6 Bonhill Street
London EC2A 4PU
United Kingdom

SAGE Publications India Pvt. Ltd.
M-32 Market
Greater Kailash I
New Delhi 110 048 India

Printed in the United States of America

Library of Congress Cataloging-in-Publication Data

Brooks-Harris, Jeff E.
  Workshops: Designing and facilitating experiential learning /
by Jeff E. Brooks-Harris & Susan R. Stock-Ward.
    p. cm.
  Includes bibliographical references and index.
  ISBN 0-7619-1020-4 (cloth: acid-free paper).
  ISBN 0-7619-1021-2 (pbk.: acid-free paper)
    1. Forums (Discussion and debate)—Planning.. 2. Active learning.
  3. Experiential learning. I. Stock-Ward, Susan R. II. Title.
  III. Title: Designing and facilitating experiential learning.
  LC6519.B76   1999
  808.53—ddc21   99-6167

99 00 01 02 03 04 05 7 6 5 4 3 2 1

Acquiring Editor:	Jim Nageotte
Editorial Assistant:	Heidi Van Middlesworth
Production Editor:	Wendy Westgate
Editorial Assistant:	Nevair Kabakian
Typesetter/Designer:	Marion Warren
Cover Designer:	Candice Harman

Contents

Preface   xv

Introduction: Three Lessons From *The Wizard of Oz*   xvii
   Purpose of This Book   xviii
   Theory Into Practice   xviii
   How to Use This Book   xix

1. Toward an Integrated Model of Workshop
Design and Facilitation   1
   Reflecting on Workshop Learning   2
   Workshop Definitions and Emphases   2
    Historical Definitions   2
    Workshop Emphases   3
    A New Definition   6
    When Is a Workshop Not a Workshop?   6
    The Facilitator Role   7
   Experiential Learning   8
   Applying Kolb's Model to Workshop Development   10
    Workshop Development Tasks   10
    Using Learning Styles to Understand Workshop Participants   11
    Using Experiential Learning Processes to Design Workshops   12
    Using Workshop Facilitation Skills to Encourage Experiential
     Learning   13

An Integrated Model of Workshop Development   14

Summary   15

Planning for Application   15

2. **Using Learning Styles to Understand Participants and Guide Workshop Design**   **19**

Reflecting on Your Own Learning Needs   20

Understanding Workshop Participants: Two Design
  Strategies   21
  Something for Everyone   21
  Measure and Match   21

Kolb's Model of Learning Styles   22
  Theory   22
  Application to Workshops   25

Dunn and Dunn's Model of Learning Styles   26
  Theory   26
  Application to Workshops   27

Jung's Model of Psychological Type   30
  Theory   30
  Application to Workshops   31

Other Factors That Impact Workshop Learning   35
  Gender   35
  Culture   36

Summary   37

Planning for Application   37

3. **Preparing for Workshop Design: Gathering Information and Setting Goals**   **39**

Reflecting on Preparation   40

Preparation Time and Effort   40

Gathering Preliminary Information   41
  Who Is Initiating This Workshop?   41
  Who Else Is Invested in the Workshop?   42
  Who Will Be Attending the Workshop?   43
  What Are the Topic, Title, and Content of the Workshop?   44
  Why Is the Workshop Being Requested or Offered?   45
  When Will the Workshop Be Offered?   45

How Long Will the Workshop Last?   45
Where Will the Workshop Take Place?   46
What Arrangements Will Be Made? By Whom?   46

Negotiating a Workshop Agreement   47

Determining the Needs of Workshop Participants   48
Formal Needs Assessment   49
Needs Prediction   51
Assessment Within Workshops   51
Determining the Needs of the Requester and Other
    Stakeholders   52
Customizing Learning to the Needs of a Group   53
What Kinds of Needs Should Be Determined?   53

Setting Goals and Learning Objectives   55
Goals   55
Learning Objectives   55
Content Versus Learning Process Objectives   56

Choosing Additional Resources   57
Types of Resources   57
Using Resources to Promote Experiential Learning   57

Summary   59

Planning for Application   59

4. Creating a Comprehensive Workshop Design   **61**

Reflecting on Workshop Design   62

Choosing a Consistent Theme   62

Beginning and Ending Your Workshop   63

Including Different Types of Learning Activities   64
Reflecting-on-Experience Activities   64
Assimilating and Conceptualizing Activities   66
Experimenting and Practicing Activities   67
Planning-for-Application Activities   68

Sequencing Learning Activities   68
Kolb's Cycle of Learning   68
Alternate Workshop Sequences   69
Other Strategies for Sequencing Activities   70

Designing Workshops of Different Lengths   71

Sample Workshop Outline   72

Summary   72

Planning for Application   74

5. **Designing Effective Workshop Learning Activities**   **75**

     Reflecting on Workshop Activities   76

     What Are Learning Activities?   76

     Beginning to Design Learning Activities   77

     Designing Reflecting-on-Experience Activities   78

     Designing Assimilating and Conceptualizing Activities   81

     Designing Experimenting and Practicing Activities   82

     Designing Planning-for-Application Activities   83

     Specific Examples of Learning Activities   84

     Examples of Reflecting Activities   84

         Icebreakers   84

         Dyadic or Small-Group Sharing   84

         Stimulus Role-Plays   85

         Gallery Exercises   85

         Brainstorming   86

         Guided Fantasies   86

         Games   87

         Storytelling   87

         Music   88

     Examples of Assimilating Activities   88

         Lectures/Lecturettes   88

         Group Surveys   88

         Values Clarification   89

         Questionnaires/Instruments   89

         Modeling Role-Plays   90

         Case Studies   90

         Movement/Sorting   90

         Fishbowl Discussions   91

         Read-Arounds   91

         Handouts/Overheads   92

         Videos   92

     Examples of Experimenting Activities   92

         Practice Role-Plays   92

         Simulations   93

Worksheets 93
Card Sorting 94
Open Discussions 94
Structured Discussions 94
Artwork 95
Scenarios 95
Maps 96
Time Lines 96
Psychodrama 96
Check-In/Check Out 97

Examples of Planning Activities 97
Personal Practice of Skills Learned in Role-Plays 97
Action Plans 98
Goal Setting 98
Brainstorming Solutions 99
Homework 99
Quizzes 99
Speak-Outs 100

Adaptation of Activities 100

Summary 100

Planning for Application 101

6. **Directing the Workshop and Creating a Learning Environment** **103**

Reflecting on Workshop Direction 104

The Workshop Learning Environment 104
Arranging the Physical Environment 105
Creating Relationships 106
Multidirectional Communication 108
Building Trust and Acceptance 108
Providing Encouragement 109

Beginning the Workshop 110
Introduction and Welcome 110
Overview of the Workshop 112

Maintaining a Coherent Workshop Message 114

Pacing and Timing 115

Concluding the Workshop 116
Reviewing Content to Consolidate Learning 116

Planning for the Future	116
Feedback/Evaluations	117
Follow-Up	117
Summary	117
Planning for Application	118

7. Facilitation Skills for Different Types of Experiential Learning — **119**

Assessing Your Facilitation Skills	120
Four Types of Facilitation Skills	122
Engaging Facilitation Skills	122
Informing Facilitation Skills	123
Involving Facilitation Skills	124
Applying Facilitation Skills	124
Your Facilitation Preferences	124
Experimenting With Facilitation Skills	125
Cofacilitation Skills	126
Examples of Facilitation Skills	127
Examples of Engaging Facilitation Skills	127
Previewing Workshop Content or Goals	127
Setting Ground Rules or Group Norms	128
Reflecting	128
Paraphrasing	128
Reinforcing	129
Asking for More Information	129
Questioning	129
Probing	129
Challenging Assumptions	130
Bouncing Questions Back to the Group	130
Encouraging Brainstorming	130
Self-Disclosure That Increases Motivation	130
Examples of Informing Facilitation Skills	131
Clarifying Assumptions	131
Giving Information	131
Surveying	131
Answering Questions	132
Clarifying	132
Pointing Out What Was Not Mentioned	132
Identifying Themes	132

    Modeling New Behavior 133
    Punch Lines 133
    Summarizing 133
    Explaining 133
    Self-Disclosure That Provides Information 134

  Examples of Involving Facilitation Skills 134
    Prompting Participation 134
    Encouraging New Behavior Within the Workshop 134
    Encouraging Direct Interaction/"Directing Traffic" 135
    Connecting One Person's Ideas With Another's 135
    Interpreting 135
    Process Observation 136
    Immediacy 136
    Asking for Feedback 136
    Encouraging Interpersonal Feedback 137
    Asking for Reactions to an Activity 137
    Focusing/Getting Back on Track 137

  Examples of Applying Facilitation Skills 138
    Encouraging New Behavior Outside the Workshop 138
    Generalizing From One Environment to Another 138
    Exploring the Future 138
    Pointing Out Opportunities for Application 138
    Encouraging Action 139
    Encouraging Goal Setting 139
    Assigning Homework 139
    Brainstorming Solutions 139
    Self-Disclosure That Models Application 140

  Summary 140

  Planning for Application 140

8. Workshop Evaluations: Strategies,
Variables, and Plans **143**

  Reflecting on Workshop Evaluation 144

  Why Should You Evaluate Your Workshops? 144
    Purpose 144
    Audience 145
    Evaluator 145

  Choosing an Evaluation Strategy 146
    Formative or Summative Strategies 146
    Quantitative or Qualitative Strategies 147

Formal or Informal Strategies 147
Combining Strategies 148

Deciding Which Variables to Measure 148
Evaluating Satisfaction 149
Objective-Based Evaluation 150

Developing an Evaluation Plan 152
Formulating Questions and Standards 152
Selecting a Research Design 153
Collecting Information 153
Analyzing Information 154
Reporting Information 155

Summary 155

Planning for Application 156

9. Improving Your Workshop Design, Directing, and Facilitation Skills **157**

Reflecting on Your Workshop Skills 158

Sources of Information 158
Self-Evaluation 158
Your Cofacilitator 159
Ask a Peer to Observe 159
Ask for Feedback From the Requester 159
Attend Other Workshops 160

Improving Your Workshop Skills 160

Improving Your Workshop Design Skills 161
Reviewing Design Skills 161
Rating Your Workshop Design Skills 163
Experimenting With Design Skills 163
Using New Design Skills 164

Improving Your Workshop Directing Skills 165
Reviewing Directing Skills 165
Rating Your Directing Skills 166
Experimenting With Directing Skills 166

Improving Your Facilitation Skills 168
Reviewing Facilitation Skills 168
Rating Your Facilitation Skills 169
Experimenting With Facilitation Skills 171

Summary   173
  Planning for Application   173

References   175

Index   181

About the Authors   187

To my mother, Jeanne, and to the memory of my father, Dewey,
who taught me to feel deeply and think critically;
and to my wife Carolyn and my daughter Genevieve,
who fill my life with joy.

—J. B.-H.

To Mike and to my family, for their encouragement and tolerance
of me during the process of writing this book.

—S. R. S.

Preface

The ideas in this book were developed over the past several years through attempts to clarify for ourselves and to teach others the fine art of workshop design and facilitation. The central concept of using a theory of learning styles to classify and organize workshop activities and facilitation skills felt more like a discovery than an invention. What had previously been a loose collection of ideas was suddenly transformed into a coherent model just a few weeks before a presentation at a national conference.

Jeff is thankful for all he learned from numerous workshop teachers, cofacilitators, participants, and trainees with whom he has collaborated at Ohio State University, the University of Utah, Southern Illinois University, and the University of Hawai'i. Jeff gives special thanks to Robbie Geist and Lori Davis, who copresented an early version of this approach, and to Sharon Nance, who added the crucial element of learning styles and began the process of writing the book with him. Jeff's mother, Jeanne Harris, and his wife, Carolyn Brooks-Harris, both provided valuable editing, for which he is grateful. Jeff is most greatly indebted to his friend and colleague Sue for coming aboard as co-captain when this extroverted author almost let the boat sink for lack of companionship.

Sue thanks the supervisors of her early workshop efforts, Howie Schein and Pat Robinson, for helping her begin her interest in this area. She also thanks her colleagues at Marquette University and especially those at the University of Akron for their support of the concepts within the book as well as the writing of the book itself. Sue is grateful to Jeff for inviting her to coauthor this project, for learning with her how to work on such a joint effort, and especially for his colleagueship and friendship. Lastly, she thanks the workshop trainees and participants with whom she has had the good fortune to work over the past decade.

Both of our editors, Armand Lauffer and Jim Nageotte, have been very supportive and helped us through the tricky waters of writing our first book. Our spouses, families, colleagues, and friends have been patient and supportive and still asked about the book's progress even when it took so long to complete.

Introduction

Three Lessons From
The Wizard of Oz

Reflect with us on a movie with which most of you are familiar—*The Wizard of Oz* (LeRoy & Fleming, 1939). It offers three lessons that have direct application to workshop design and facilitation. In one of the final scenes, Dorothy and her three friends return to the Wizard after defeating the Wicked Witch of the West and ask that their wishes be granted as he had promised. Dorothy wants to go home to Kansas; the Scarecrow wants a brain; the Tin Woodsman wants a heart; and the Cowardly Lion wants courage. Therein lies our first lesson: *"Although they may all participate in a shared activity, individuals are likely to have different needs."* Workshop participants are likely to have different learning styles.

Dorothy and her friends soon discover that the Wizard, rather than being all-powerful, is a mere mortal with a great multimedia projection system. Luckily, he's also a great improviser. Reaching into his carpetbag, he presents each of the characters with symbols of their learning that represent the fulfillment of their wishes. The Tin Woodsman is given a pocket watch in the shape of a heart to honor his compassion. The Scarecrow receives a diploma to recognize his intelligence. The Wizard awards the Cowardly Lion with a medal of courage. He even offers to take Dorothy back to

Kansas in a balloon. Here's our second lesson: *If you are not an all-powerful wizard, it helps to have a bag of useful items to help you out in a bind.* When applied to workshop planning, this lesson suggests that it is important to offer individually designed rewards to meet the needs of different individuals. In a workshop environment, these rewards come in the form of appropriate learning experiences that stimulate different types of learners.

Interestingly, the Wizard did not actually grant the wishes of Dorothy and her friends, yet all were able to gain what they needed. How did they attain these aspirations? Through experience! The Tin Woodsman found his heart by being in a situation that required compassion. By responding with quick thinking, the Scarecrow recognized his brain. Protecting his friends from danger allowed the Cowardly Lion to find his courage. Dorothy eventually realized that she had had the power to go home all along. Our third lesson from *The Wizard of Oz* is this: *"Individuals learn best through experience."* If we can create an active and experiential learning environment, then it is possible to encourage workshop learners to recognize their own compassion, intelligence, and courage, and to take this learning home with them!

Purpose of This Book

Our purpose is to present a model of workshop design and facilitation based on how different people think and learn. The model is organized around a theory that describes both experiential learning and individual learning styles. This model will help you understand workshop participants, design a comprehensive workshop, and use effective facilitation skills. We describe a systematic approach to workshop design and provide dozens of examples of activities that can be applied to virtually any topic. You will be given tools that will allow you to recognize your strengths as a workshop presenter and to address areas of relative weakness. We believe that we are providing you with an integrated and practical approach to workshop development that you will find engaging, informative, and beneficial.

Theory Into Practice

The workshop model described here represents the application of learning theory to the practice of workshop design and facilitation that has been tested by experience. The model has been very useful to our practice, that of dozens of students and interns we've trained, and hundreds of professionals to whom we have presented at conferences. The learning theories on which we have drawn have been tested in other settings, but very little research has been conducted on the impact of workshops and other developmental interventions (Drum & Lawler, 1988). Therefore, one limitation of this model is that many of the assertions that we make are actually hypotheses rather than empirically established facts. For example, we assert throughout the book that certain types of learners will prefer and benefit from certain types of workshop activities. We want to acknowledge that this is an assumption based on theory and practice that has not been scientifically validated. We hope that practitioners will value and use what we have shared and that researchers may take an interest in the area of workshops and begin to test some of these ideas in the future.

How to Use This Book

Just as different workshop participants have different learning needs, so do workshop designers and facilitators. Your learning style, level of experience, and unique interests will determine how and what you will want to learn from this book. We have written the book with the assumption that some of the readers are new to workshops and that others are experienced facilitators. If you are a new workshop presenter with little or no previous experience, then you may want to read the whole book in order to be exposed to the entire process of workshop development. If you already have workshop experience or have read other books on the subject and want to see what we have to say that is new and different, you may want to go directly to the unique aspects of our model. These are described in the last section of Chapter 1, in Chapter 2 (participants), Chapters 4 and 5 (design), and Chapter 7 (facilitation skills). If there is a particular part of workshop development that it is most important for you to learn about right away, you may want to read the overview of the model at the end of Chapter 1 and then proceed to the chapter that corresponds to your needs. For example, if you need to design a workshop next week and want new ideas for learning activities, you may want to move on to Chapter 5 after Chapter 1.

In keeping with our advocacy for active learning in workshops, we encourage your active participation in this book as well. Following the introduction of each chapter, we ask you to reflect on your own experience and to bring this learning with you as you read the chapter. We address both novice and veteran workshop presenters. If you have not presented workshops before, you will be able to reflect on your experience teaching or presenting in other educational contexts or on your experience as a learner. There are also times throughout the chapters that we ask you to engage in active learning. We include exercises that help you experiment with and practice the concepts and skills we describe. Other chapters have questions (beginning with arrows) within the text to encourage you to pause and think about how the information presented can be related to your own situation. At the end of each chapter, we ask you to plan to apply the ideas to your own future workshops.

We both find workshop design and facilitation an exciting and rewarding part of our professional lives. It is our desire that, through this book, we are able to communicate some of our enthusiasm. We hope that you are able to use many of the ideas we have presented and that this learning helps you become a more effective and confident workshop presenter. Thank you for your interest in our model and good luck with your workshops!

Chapter

1

Toward an Integrated Model of Workshop Design and Facilitation

Workshops provide environments for learning to occur in a dynamic and powerful manner. The workshop format can be used to promote personal growth, teach professional skills, or create change within existing systems. Workshops provide an effective short-term training method that can be used in a wide array of settings with an infinite number of topics. Because of their short duration, workshops are flexible and cost-effective; they can be easily designed or modified to meet the needs of different groups and organizations. This adaptability to a particular group and topic can be employed to capture the motivation of learners and to enhance the opportunity for long-term change. Workshops have even been referred to as the "workhorse of adult and continuing education" (Fleming, 1997, p. 1) because a workhorse performs "dependably under heavy or prolonged use" (*American Heritage Dictionary,* 1992, p. 2057).

Previous ideas about workshops will be reviewed before introducing our model of workshop design and facilitation. We begin by describing historical definitions and identifying workshop characteristics and emphases and conclude with our own workshop definition, which will guide the rest of the book. Second, we will highlight the importance of the facilitator role of a workshop presenter. Third, Kolb's (1984) model of experiential learning, which forms the theoretical basis for much of the book, is introduced.

The chapter closes with the application of Kolb's model to workshop development and a description of the integrated model that results. This integrated model of workshop design and facilitation forms the foundation for all of the material that is explored in subsequent chapters.

Reflecting on Workshop Learning

As you begin to think about workshops, we invite you to reflect on your experience with learning environments by answering the following questions:

1. How would you define the word *workshop*? What makes a workshop a workshop? How does a workshop differ from a class, lecture, seminar, presentation, or discussion?

2. What was the best workshop (or other learning experience) in which you have participated? What made this experience positive?

3. What was the least effective workshop (or other learning experience) you ever attended? What made it so bad?

Workshop Definitions and Emphases

Historical Definitions

When the word *workshop* is used to refer to an educational or training format, the word is being used as an analogy. Originally, a workshop was a place where things were made and sold. A cobbler's workshop was a place where shoes were made and repaired as well as sold. It can be inferred, therefore, that when educators started using the term to describe a particular type of learning environment, it was meant to convey some of the characteristics of the original word. If this logic is followed, it can be assumed

EXHIBIT 1.1
Definitional Characteristics of Workshops

Short-Term Intensive Learning
Small Group Interaction
Active Involvement
Development of Competence
Problem Solving
Behavior Change as an Outcome
Application of New Learning

---

that a workshop is a place where work occurs, where tools are used to accomplish this work, where things may be repaired, and where the work may result in a particular product or outcome. We invite you to think about your own role as an educator or trainer and to keep in mind the origin of the term *workshop* as you develop your own "tools" in this "work."

Fleming (1997) recently provided a definition of workshops that emphasized the development of competence, interactive learning among participants, opportunities for hands-on practice, practical and intensive interaction, small-group work, and application of new learning. Earlier definitions of workshops also identified similar themes. Morgan, Holmes, and Bundy (1963) pointed out that "as the word implies, a workshop means work" (p. 61) and highlighted the importance of small groups, complete participation, and behavior change in workshop learning. Sork (1984) defined a workshop as "a relatively short-term, intensive, problem-focused learning experience that actively involves participants in the identification and analysis of problems and in the development and evaluation of solutions" (p. 5). The important elements of these definitions are summarized in Exhibit 1.1.

Workshop Emphases

These workshop definitions offer different emphases. For example, Fleming (1997) emphasized the development of competence (which we will refer to as skill building), whereas Sork (1984) emphasized problem solving as an essential feature of workshops. Our model recognizes skill building and problem solving as two valid workshop goals but also recog-

EXHIBIT 1.2

Possible Workshop Emphases

Problem Solving

Skill Building

Increasing Knowledge

Systemic Change

Personal Awareness/Self-Improvement

---

nizes other emphases such as systemic change, increased knowledge, and personal awareness or self-improvement. These different emphases are listed in Exhibit 1.2, and each is discussed and exemplified.

Skill Building

Skill-building workshops aim to equip participants with specific skills that they can use in their work or personal lives. The facilitator of a skill-building workshop may have more expertise than participants but there is still an attempt to promote interpersonal learning and hands-on practice. For example, workshops might address management skills, computer use, assertiveness, gardening, or parenting skills.

Problem Solving

Problem-solving workshops bring together people with knowledge that they can share with one another to find new solutions to problems. For example, a group of teachers, administrators, and researchers might work together to find new strategies for preventing violence in schools.

Increasing Knowledge

Increasing knowledge also can be the emphasis of a workshop. However, if knowledge is only transmitted in a didactic fashion, it is considered a lecture and does not fit our definition of a workshop. Although most workshops do result in increased knowledge, they also provide opportunities for participants to use and apply their newfound knowledge. For example, a workshop can be used to inform physicians of the results of new cancer research. For this educational experience to be an experiential workshop, the participants would need to be provided with the opportunity to practice using their new knowledge in diagnosis and to prepare to apply the knowledge in treatment settings.

Systemic Change

Systemic change is another possible emphasis for workshops. Such workshops often fall into the context of consultation or organizational development. For example, a sexual harassment workshop might be offered within a company after there have been reports of harassment. The aim of the workshop would be to change attitudes and behaviors within the workplace in order to create a more positive environment for all of the company's employees.

Personal Awareness/Self-Improvement

Personal awareness, self-improvement, or both, are the goals for other workshops. These may focus on issues like self-esteem or positive thinking and promote change by helping participants become aware of their own thoughts, attitudes, or feelings and by helping people make positive changes in their lives.

Interaction Among Emphases

It should be pointed out that these emphases may overlap substantially with one another. Rarely is it possible to isolate a process like awareness from related emphases like skill building or problem solving. For example, a workshop that promotes personal awareness in an area such as self-esteem frequently will be tied to skill building in an area such as assertiveness. It is our expectation that most workshops will include more than one of these emphases and some may address all five.

➤ *In the workshops you plan to present, are you most likely to emphasize skill building, problem solving, increasing knowledge, systemic change, or personal awareness and self-improvement?*

A New Definition

In addition to these characteristics (Exhibit 1.1) and emphases (Exhibit 1.2), the workshop model we describe emphasizes three interrelated elements: experiential learning, sensitivity to different learning styles, and the use of a variety of learning activities. The following definition will be used:

A workshop is a short-term learning experience that encourages active, experiential learning and uses a variety of learning activities to meet the needs of diverse learners.

We see workshops as an ideal way to address the needs of individuals with different learning preferences through the use of a variety of teaching and learning approaches. Throughout the remainder of the book, increasingly specific information about learning styles, learning activities, and facilitation skills will be provided to help you create an effective workshop learning environment that is sensitive and responsive to diverse learners.

Because definitions are not used consistently, there may be other short-term educational or training formats that promote experiential learning. These formats may be called training programs, presentations, or seminars. For conceptual clarity, we would consider these workshops if there is active learning using a variety of methods to meet the needs of diverse learners. If the program format allows only one-way communication and does not promote participant involvement, such as the exclusive use of a lecture format, it would not meet our definition of a workshop.

When Is a Workshop Not a Workshop?

Have you ever attended a workshop that was really a lecture? While preparing this book, one of us attended nine 2-hour programs described as "workshops" during a 4-day conference. Of these nine, three were exclusively lectures with no attempt to provide active learning; three included videotaped or live demonstrations; one had participants respond in writing to material presented by the facilitator; and only two had participants break down into small groups for interactive learning. Although we do not question the value of lectures and demonstrations, these elements alone do not fit our definition of a workshop. The program that included participants responding to material in writing took an important step toward active learning (it might be noted that the presenter was speaking to an audience of over 1,000 and it was impressive that he had found a way to include an active exercise at all). However, only the two programs that included participant interaction met the definition of *workshop* provided here.

➤ *How would you define the word* workshop? *How does your definition differ from the one presented here?*

The Facilitator Role

In order to enact this vision of a workshop, it is important for the presenter to act as a facilitator of experiential learning rather than merely as a teacher or instructor. More than any other aspect of the workshop environment, the participants will be impacted by *you* as a person. When creating an interpersonal learning environment, you as the facilitator are often more important than the content. *You* are your most important tool!

When the word *facilitator* is used rather than teacher, instructor, leader, or trainer, it "implies a different approach to teaching and learning that deserves validation" (Hentschel, 1997, p. 87). These implications are critical to understanding the workshop environment and the experiential learning that occurs within a workshop. Many traditional educational formats depend upon the instructor or teacher to act primarily as an expert source of information.

A workshop facilitator can stretch beyond the expert role by also encouraging learning between and among the participants, as well as through participatory experience. This expanded role can be more effective because it promotes learning on many different levels. The role of creating powerful learning experiences and guiding and encouraging personal and interpersonal learning can create change that complements and creates greater and deeper learning than merely providing information.

Your initial reactions to the idea of experiential learning and the facilitator role may include resistance; you may wish to defend traditional didactic, content-oriented instruction. For example, when this workshop model was presented to one group, a participant earnestly suggested that, "When there is so much material to be covered, we don't have time to create an engaging environment or to facilitate active involvement." People who do not see the value of experiential education may be depending upon a traditional educational paradigm. Embracing experiential learning as a valuable endeavor may require a paradigm shift (Kuhn, 1970).

A traditional unidirectional, content-based learning paradigm has dominated Western ideas of education for centuries. This paradigm is so pervasive that it can be difficult to see beyond it. Experiential education and the accompanying facilitator role represent a paradigm shift that can revolutionize the way people learn. Although the idea of experiential education has been discussed for the past two or three decades, there is still considerable resistance based on adherence to a traditional educational paradigm. An important paradigm shift for workshop facilitators is the shift in the perception of their own role as educators. A facilitator is likely to value experience and growth as much as knowledge and attend as much to process as content. A facilitator is likely to be an encourager and a colearner as well as a teacher. Facilitation of learning is often more informal and multidirectional than traditional instruction. For example, in response to a question, a traditional instructor might choose to offer her or his expertise, whereas a facilitator might choose to "bounce" the question back to the group and ask other participants what they think.

When educating people about a new topic as a traditional instructor, you might start by collecting as much information as possible and plan on spending most of the time lecturing from this material. In contrast, if you assume the role of an experiential facilitator, you might identify a key theoretical framework or set of facts but not limit yourself to focusing on this content alone. As a workshop facilitator, you might also identify ways to encourage participants to reflect on their own experience in order to increase motivation, design ways for people to experiment and practice using their newfound knowledge, and ensure that participants are prepared to apply what they have learned. As a facilitator, you will provide opportunities for interaction, feedback, and making choices so that learning is active and individualized. This expanded role of educator as facilitator is a key ingredient of experiential learning. Later, we will further define the roles played by a workshop presenter by making a distinction between "designing," "directing," and "facilitating."

➤ *What parts of the facilitator role do you already do well? What could you do to enhance the role of facilitation in the workshops that you present?*

Experiential Learning

We have identified experience as a crucial aspect of workshop learning. Therefore, a model of experiential learning has been selected to inform and direct our considerations. We will draw most heavily on the theory described by David Kolb (1984) because it has a crucial advantage over other models. There are many models that describe learning cycles. For example, Palmer (1981) summarized six models (including an earlier version of Kolb's model) that describe distinct stages of learning organized as a cycle. Likewise, there are many different theories that describe individual differences related to human learning. However, Kolb's model is most useful in our consideration of workshops because it describes both individual learning styles that can be used to understand workshop participants and a cycle of learning that can be used to organize workshop activities and facilitation skills. In addition, Kolb's (1985) Learning Styles Inventory provides instrumentation to operationalize these concepts. For these reasons, we will use Kolb's model as the primary theoretical base for the approach described in this book.

David Kolb (1984) proposed a model of experiential learning in his book, *Experiential Learning: Experience as the Source of Learning and Development*. He drew upon the foundational work of Kurt Lewin in action research and laboratory training and related it to the work of John Dewey and Jean Piaget. The heart of Kolb's experiential learning model is a cycle of learning that proposes four learning modes: concrete experience, reflective observation, abstract conceptualization, and active experimentation. A key idea in Kolb's model is that experiential learning occurs most effectively when all four modes in this cycle of learning are completed. This cycle of learning is depicted in Figure 1.1.

In addition to describing learning as a cycle, Kolb (1984) also used these four modes to suggest that "there are two primary dimensions to the learning process. The first dimension represents the concrete experiencing of events at one end and abstract conceptualization at the other. The other dimension has active experimentation at one extreme and reflective observation at the other" (pp. 30-31). McCarthy (1980, 1990) labeled these continua as perception (anchored by concrete experience and abstract conceptualization) and processing (anchored by active experimentation and reflective observation). By considering the ways that different people perceive and process, individual learning styles can be identified. These two dimensions can visually serve as horizontal and vertical axes to create four quadrants that represent four individual learning styles. The concept of learning styles is another important aspect of Kolb's model that can be used to direct this consideration of workshops.

The first learning style describes Divergers (Kolb, 1984, 1985) or *Imaginative Learners* (McCarthy, 1990), who perceive primarily through concrete experience and process primarily through reflective observation. The second learning style describes Assimilators (Kolb, 1984, 1985) or *Analytic Learners* (McCarthy, 1980, 1990), who perceive primarily

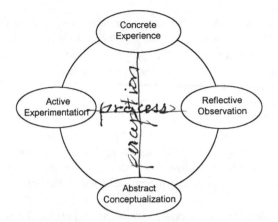

Figure 1.1. Kolb's Experiential Learning Cycle

through abstract conceptualization and process through reflective observation. Third, Convergers (Kolb, 1984, 1985) or *Common Sense Learners* (McCarthy, 1980, 1990) perceive primarily through abstract conceptualization and process primarily through active experimentation. Fourth, Accommodators (Kolb, 1984, 1985) or *Dynamic Learners* (McCarthy, 1980, 1990) perceive primarily through concrete experience and process primarily through active experimentation. These four learning styles are depicted in Figure 1.2. Both of Kolb's (1984) views of learning—as four parts of a continuous cycle and as two complementary dimensions or continua that can be used to identify learning styles—are useful to this consideration of workshop design and facilitation.

➤ *Which parts of Kolb's model of experiential learning and individual learning styles seem familiar or attractive to you? Are there parts of the model with which you disagree or that you don't like?*

Applying Kolb's Model to Workshop Development

Workshop Development Tasks

Now that Kolb's (1984) model of experiential learning has been introduced, it can be applied to the domain of workshop development. A major premise of the model presented in this book is that there are three major tasks involved in successful workshop development. The first task is

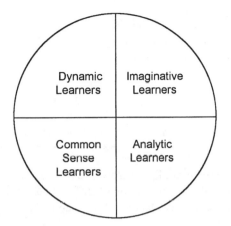

Figure 1.2. Individual Learning Styles

understanding workshop participants. The second task is developing a comprehensive workshop design that addresses the topic for a particular group of participants within a particular context. The third task is facilitating the workshop in a way that promotes active learning.

Experiential learning theory can inform us about all three of these tasks. First, when experiential learning is applied to the task of understanding a workshop audience and its individual participants, the concept of *individual learning styles* can be used to identify four clusters of learning needs and preferences. Second, in addressing workshop design, the four learning processes can be used to identify four distinct groups of adaptable learning activities that can be used to promote different types of learning. Third, four sets of *workshop facilitation skills* can be identified that correspond to the four basic learning processes. In developing a particular workshop, you might use Kolb's Learning Style Inventory to measure the needs of workshop learners and use this information to choose which activities to plan and to anticipate the types of skills you are most likely to use. These three key concepts based on experiential learning theory and their correspondence to workshop development tasks are highlighted in Exhibit 1.3.

Using Learning Styles to Understand Workshop Participants

The integrated workshop model described here uses Kolb's four learning styles as a primary method for understanding workshop participants. Individual learning styles can be used to measure the needs of a specific group

EXHIBIT 1.3
Workshop Development Tasks and Key Concepts

Task	Key Concept
Understanding Participants	Individual Learning Styles
Workshop Design	Adaptable Learning Activities
Workshop Facilitation	Workshop Facilitation Skills

of participants, or the idea of learning styles can be used as a guide to design a workshop that will meet the needs of different learners. Both of these strategies will be more fully elaborated in Chapter 2.

Using Experiential Learning
Processes to Design Workshops

To guide the workshop design process, we have identified four experiential learning processes that correspond to the four learning styles. We will refer to these four learning processes as reflecting on experience, assimilating and conceptualizing, experimenting and practicing, and planning for application. These four experiential learning processes are depicted in Figure 1.3 and are briefly described here.

First, reflecting on experience occurs when learners are encouraged to recall important aspects of their past experience. This process increases motivation and prepares participants for learning by reminding them of what they already know (Kolb, 1984). An assertiveness workshop might start by having participants share with one another times they wish they had been more assertive.

Second, assimilating and conceptualizing moves learners from reflection and observation to abstract conceptualization. Assimilating and conceptualizing may include more didactic teaching but also encourages participants to compare the didactic material to their own experience. A leadership workshop includes the facilitators' performing a role-play in order to demonstrate common mistakes that leaders make and then encourages participants to identify the errors and suggest alternative behaviors.

Third, experimenting and practicing encourages learners to move from abstract conceptualization to active experimentation. In this process, learners are asked to use new knowledge actively and practice skills in an experimental way. For example, in a sexual harassment workshop, partici-

Figure 1.3. Experiential Learning Processes

pants are given scenarios printed on index cards and asked to sort each into one of three piles based on whether they think harassment did not occur or whether the scenario constituted a hostile environment or quid pro quo harassment.

Fourth, planning for application prepares learners to move from active experimentation back to concrete experience. Much of the process of application occurs, by necessity, outside of a workshop in one's professional or personal life and therefore this process emphasizes planning and preparation. At the end of a writing workshop, participants might be given time to write an outline for the next piece they plan to write.

To design a comprehensive workshop, you can use learning activities that encourage each of these four types of learning. Using these four processes accomplishes two important goals. First, you provide different learning experiences that meet the primary needs of participants with different learning styles. Second, you create a learning experience that creates a complete cycle of learning that deepens learning for all participants. Designing effective activities that represent each of these learning processes is the topic of Chapter 5.

Using Workshop Facilitation Skills to Encourage Experiential Learning

In the same way that we use learning styles to identify workshop learning processes, we also use learning styles quadrants to identify four

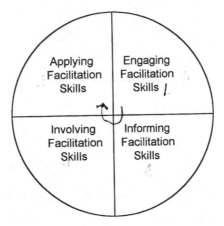

Figure 1.4. Workshop Facilitation Skills

types of workshop facilitation microskills. The facilitation skills that are related to reflecting on experience and the imaginative learning style are referred to as *engaging facilitation skills* because an important role of the facilitator is to help the participants engage in experiential learning. The skills that correspond to assimilating and conceptualizing and the analytic learning style are called *informing facilitation skills* and highlight the role of facilitator as a provider of information. Skills that are related to experimenting and practicing and the common sense learning style are called *involving facilitation skills* because of the importance of actively involving participants in the process of experimentation. The last set of skills, which corresponds to planning for application and the dynamic learning style, are called *applying facilitation skills*. These four types of workshop facilitation skills are depicted in Figure 1.4. These skills will be explored in greater detail in Chapter 7.

An Integrated Model of Workshop Development

Now that we have used Kolb's (1984) model of learning styles and experiential learning to understand three workshop development tasks, we can combine these three applications into one integrated model. We have used Kolb's four quadrants to understand participants' learning styles (Figure 1.2), to identify learning processes that guide workshop design by suggesting four types of activities (Figure 1.3), and to identify four types of workshop facilitation skills (Figure 1.4). When these three components are combined, the result is an integrated model of workshop development that organizes 12 elements into three complementary cycles. This integrated model of workshop development is illustrated in Figure 1.5.

As you view the integrated model, remember that the four quadrants in each circle correspond to one another. For example, the needs of Imaginative Learners (upper right quadrant) correspond to the process of reflecting on experience and to engaging facilitation skills. The primary needs of Imaginative Learners are met through reflecting on experience and are encouraged by engaging skills. For example, reflecting activities like icebreakers or brainstorming (see Chapter 5) may be particularly appealing to Imaginative Learners and may require the facilitator to use engaging facilitation skills like paraphrasing, reinforcing, or bouncing questions back to the group (see Chapter 7). This same correspondence is true for the other three quadrants as well.

➤ *Which parts of this workshop model seem familiar or attractive to you? Are there parts that you do not like or that do not fit your style as a workshop presenter?*

Summary

This chapter reviewed past ideas about workshops and experiential learning. A new definition was proposed and possible workshop emphases and the importance of the facilitator role were identified. Kolb's model of experiential learning was introduced and applied to the tasks of understanding participants, designing a comprehensive workshop, and using effective facilitation skills. The result is an integrated model of workshop development. Although the presentation of this model concludes this chapter, it also introduces the rest of the book. Each of the elements of the integrated model will be explored in more detail in subsequent chapters.

Planning for Application

The following questions will encourage you to apply the ideas in this chapter to your current or future role as a workshop designer and facilitator.

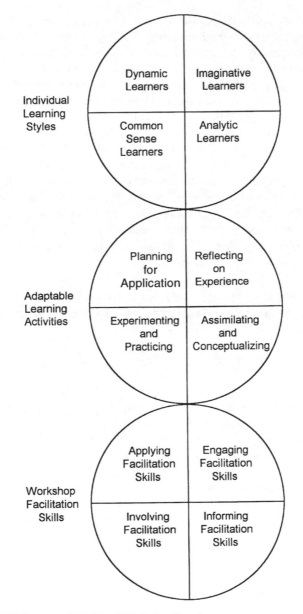

Figure 1.5. Integrated Model of Workshop Development

1. In the workshops that you plan for the future, please identify ways that you might address the following emphases:

   a. Problem Solving

   _____

   b. Skill Building

   _____

   c. Increasing Knowledge

   _____

   d. Systemic Change

   _____

   e. Personal Awareness/Self-Improvement

   _____

2. Please think about workshop activities with which you are already familiar and identify those that promote each of the following experiential learning processes:

   a. Reflecting on Experience

   _____

   b. Assimilating and Conceptualizing

   _____

   c. Experimenting and Practicing

   _____

   d. Planning for Application

   _____

2

Using Learning Styles to Understand Participants and Guide Workshop Design

One key to being a successful gardener is knowing that different plants need different conditions to thrive. Some plants need lots of water, others need little; some need direct sunlight, others need shade; some plants need fertilizer, others don't. The same is true of individual learners, each of whom has different needs and preferences. To be a successful workshop facilitator, you will recognize individual variations in learning styles and respond to these differences with conducive environments and activities. In this way, the learners in your garden will grow and flourish.

To design and facilitate a workshop that appeals to and addresses learners' diverse needs, you will consider the impact of individual learning styles. Most of us have ideas and impressions about how we, ourselves, learn best and what we prefer in new learning situations. As a workshop facilitator, however, you may have 30 participants with strongly held learning preferences that differ from yours and from one another's. The challenge is to use knowledge of learning styles to design a workshop that is responsive to all of these participants' needs.

We have organized our approach to designing and facilitating workshops around David Kolb's (1984) model of experiential learning and learning styles. Of course, Kolb's model is only one of many that could be used to direct our thinking. In order to demonstrate the broad usefulness of the idea of learning styles, we will review Kolb's model, as well as two others, and discuss the implications of each model for workshops. We conclude the chapter by briefly looking at gender and cultural differences.

Reflecting on Your Own Learning Needs

Please reflect on the following questions, which will help you think about your own individual learning needs and preferences:

1. Do you prefer to learn by listening and observing, or by actively participating?

   _____

2. Do you prefer to learn new information by reading or viewing it, by listening to it delivered verbally, by writing, or through active movement?

   _____

3. Would you prefer to learn by thinking through things on your own, or by interacting with other learners?

   _____

These questions preview concepts from three models that we use to stimulate thinking about workshop participants and workshop design. The first question corresponds to the distinction between reflective observation and active experimentation (Kolb, 1984). The second focuses on the differences between visual, auditory, tactile, and kinesthetic learning (Dunn & Dunn, 1993). The distinction between extroversion and introversion (Jung, 1971a) is previewed by the third question. These are but a few of the participant differences appearing in workshops that can be used to guide design.

Understanding Workshop
Participants: Two Design Strategies

Exploring different ways to respond to individual differences has led us to identify two strategies for workshop design: "Something for Everyone" and "Measure and Match." These strategies will be described and then combined with three different models of learning styles.

Something for Everyone

The something-for-everyone strategy begins with the assumption that you will have a variety of learners in your workshop group and that you should select learning activities that correspond to all of their needs. This strategy does not require measuring the needs of participants ahead of time but does involve using a specific theory or model to guide your design. The model that you use as a guide can be a general description of learning (such as the three models described later in this chapter) or a theory that is more closely related to the content of the workshop. For example, to apply the something-for-everyone strategy to a workshop on management, you can utilize a model that describes different management styles and select activities that will correspond to the needs of each style. In this way, you are ensuring that your design will attend to the preferences of all participants. The advantage of the something-for-everyone strategy is that it is easy to use and does not require formal needs assessment. The disadvantage is that it does not allow you to customize the workshop to the specific needs of a particular group.

Measure and Match

In contrast, the measure-and-match strategy involves identifying participants before a workshop and using needs assessment methods to collect information that will guide your design. This allows you to tailor the workshop to the needs of particular learners by selecting activities that correspond to their preferences. This needs assessment can be a general measure of learning preferences or a more specific measure related to workshop content. Using the same example, to apply the measure-and-match strategy to a management workshop, you can assess the management styles of participants and tailor your design to meet the needs of the predominant style or styles in the group. The advantage of the measure-

and-match strategy is the ability to utilize accurate knowledge of individual participants' needs to design a unique learning environment. Sometimes, however, the results of a needs assessment will reveal a diversity of learning styles that will result in offering activities for all styles just as you would have done utilizing "something for everyone." The obvious disadvantage is that this strategy can be used only in situations in which you can identify participants and have them complete an instrument or survey ahead of time.

Either of these two strategies can be used with almost any theory or model related to workshop learning or content. You can decide which theory or model is most useful or most closely related to your particular topic. However, in order to take full advantage of the measure-and-match strategy, it is necessary to use an instrument in needs assessment (which is addressed more fully in Chapter 3). To exemplify these two strategies, we will review three models of learning styles and then identify ways to apply something for everyone or measure and match to each model.

➤ *For what workshop topics would it be appropriate for you to use a measure-and-match strategy? What kind of instrument can you use during needs assessment? For what workshops would it be better to use the something-for-everyone strategy? Is there a model or theory related to workshop content that would be useful to guide your design?*

Kolb's Model of Learning Styles

Theory

Kolb (1984) applied his ideas about experiential learning to the concept of individuality in learning to identify four different learning styles. He identified these based on individuals' preferences for each of four modes of the learning process: concrete experience, reflective observation, abstract conceptualization, and active experimentation. Using these modes, Kolb (1984, 1985) described four groups of learners that he referred to as Divergers, Assimilators, Convergers, and Accommodators. McCarthy (1980, 1990) applied Kolb's model to teaching and relabeled the categories as Imaginative Learners, Analytic Learners, Common Sense Learners, and Dynamic Learners (McCarthy's terms are used throughout the rest of the book). These four learning styles are depicted in Figure 2.1 and are described in more detail next.

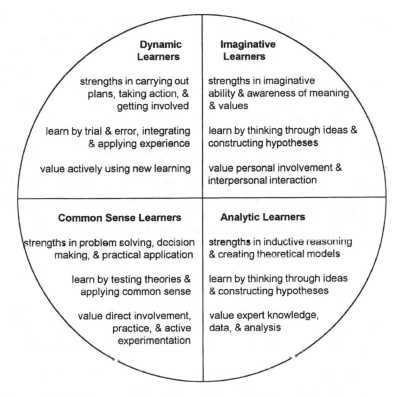

Figure 2.1. Individual Learning Styles and Learner Characteristics

Imaginative Learners are oriented toward concrete experience and reflective observation. They have strengths in imaginative ability and awareness of meaning and values (Kolb, 1984). The opportunity to reflect on their own experience as a way of personally engaging in the learning process is helpful for Imaginative Learners. These individuals want to construct personal meaning from learning. Learning environments that allow personal involvement and interpersonal interaction are a good match for Imaginative Learners (McCarthy, 1980, 1990). Imaginative Learners may particularly enjoy workshop activities that allow them to share what they already know, that allow participants to learn from one another, and that address personal values.

Analytic Learners are oriented toward abstract conceptualization and reflective observation. They have strengths in inductive reasoning and creating theoretical models (Kolb, 1984). Analytic Learners "devise theories by integrating their observations into what they know. They learn by thinking through ideas" (McCarthy, 1990, p. 32). As a result of their reflective observation, they construct hypotheses that form the basis for learning. Analytic Learners value expert knowledge and data. Traditional educational settings often allow Analytic Learners to excel because they focus on information and analysis. Workshop activities that will be particularly helpful for Analytic Learners are those that present factual information derived from research or expert opinion and that may involve data and statistics.

Common Sense Learners are oriented toward abstract conceptualization and active experimentation. They have strengths in problem solving, decision making, and practical application (Kolb, 1984). Common Sense Learners "integrate theory and practice, learning by testing theories and applying common sense" (McCarthy, 1990, p. 32). They want to put new information to immediate practical use. Common Sense Learners want to be involved in the process of hands-on learning that involves experimenting with new knowledge. A learning environment that promotes direct involvement, practice, and active experimentation is beneficial for Common Sense Learners. Workshop activities like role-plays, simulations, and worksheets encourage the hands-on experimentation that Common Sense Learners desire.

Dynamic Learners are oriented toward concrete experience and active experimentation. They have strengths related to carrying out plans, taking action, and getting involved in new experiences (Kolb, 1984). Dynamic Learners "integrate experience and application, learning by trial and error" (McCarthy, 1990, p. 32). They may be anxious to know how to apply new information to "real life." They want to take knowledge and experience with them and learn on their own, outside of traditional settings. A learning environment that builds a bridge from learning to application and points toward actively using new learning is valuable for Dynamic Learners. Brainstorming solutions, homework, action plans, and other workshop activities that anticipate the future are particularly helpful for Dynamic Learners.

In the introduction to this book, we used *The Wizard of Oz* (LeRoy & Fleming, 1939) as a metaphor to teach three lessons about workshops. The analogy can be extended to learning preferences, and the characters from the story can be used to represent the four learning styles. Imaginative Learners share something in common with the Tin Man because they want learning that appeals to their *hearts*. The Scarecrow is a symbol for Analytic

Learners who need to use their *brains*. Common Sense Learners are similar to the Cowardly Lion because it takes *courage* to try new things. Dorothy represents Dynamic Learners, who want to take their learning *home* with them.

Application to Workshops

Something for Everyone

When the something-for-everyone strategy is combined with Kolb's model and applied to workshop design, the outcome is a workshop that includes a balance of activities that correspond to each of Kolb's four learning styles. Learning activities that allow participants to recall their own past and integrate personal values into a workshop will especially appeal to Imaginative Learners. The opportunity to learn new facts and theories and apply these ideas to new areas will stimulate the thinking of Analytic Learners. Common Sense Learners will enjoy practicing new skills and experimenting in a supportive environment. A workshop that includes making concrete plans for the future is responsive to the needs of Dynamic Learners.

As you may have already noticed, the combination of the something-for-everyone strategy and Kolb's model of learning styles is the predominant approach to workshop design presented throughout this book. Designing and selecting activities that meet the needs of learners with these learning styles is addressed in Chapter 5 and will not be explored further in this chapter. However, to extend the notion that using learning styles to understand participants and guide design is not limited to this approach, other combinations of strategies and models will be explored here.

➤ *When you think about your own preferences using Kolb's model, what is your predominant learning style? As a workshop facilitator, do you tend to choose learning activities that correspond to one learning style or another? To create more balance in your workshops, are there activities that correspond to another learning style that you should emphasize more?*

Measure and Match

To combine the measure-and-match strategy with Kolb's model, you can use Kolb's Learning Style Inventory (LSI; 1985) as a part of needs assessment. The LSI is a brief, 12-item questionnaire that requires respondents to rank order four alternatives for each item. For example, the first item asks respondents to respond to the stem, "When I learn:" by ranking the following alternatives: "I like to deal with my feelings," "I like to listen and watch," "I like to think about ideas," and "I like to be doing things." When the items are completed, respondents add up their rankings on all 12 items to determine scores for each of the four dimensions. The relationship among scores on these four dimensions is used to identify an individual's preferred learning style. Advantages of the LSI include its brevity (it takes about 10 minutes to complete) and the fact that it has been empirically validated (e.g., Kolb & Wolfe, 1981; Marshall, Rice, & Cordts, 1986). By assessing the learning styles in your group, you can design a workshop that appeals to the needs of the predominant learning styles represented. If you are facilitating a communication skills workshop for a group of accountants, you might use the LSI during needs assessment and find that most of the participants are Analytic Learners. To match the needs of this group it may be necessary to provide a lot of didactic material about communication to build a conceptual foundation before experimenting with new skills that may require these participants to stretch beyond their own comfort zone.

➤ *As you think about the workshops you may present in the future, are there groups for which it would be particularly helpful to use Kolb's Learning Styles Inventory as a part of needs assessment?*

Dunn and Dunn's Model of Learning Styles

Theory

Dunn and Dunn (1993) developed a model of learning styles that addresses a wide variety of preferences related to physical environment, emotionality, sociological factors, and physiological factors including perceptual preferences. Most of Dunn and Dunn's work has focused on elementary and secondary schools, but many of their ideas are applicable to adults. We will use their ideas about sociological factors and perceptual preferences to further explore workshop design.

Sociological Factors

Sociological factors in learning styles include preferences for learning alone, in a pair, or as part of a small group or team either from peers or from an authority figure (Dunn & Dunn, 1993). Some people learn best in isolation where they can focus on their own thoughts and ideas and avoid social distractions. In contrast, others prefer to learn through interaction with another learner or with a group. Another sociological factor is whether people prefer to learn from peers of equal status or from an authority figure such as a teacher or workshop facilitator.

Perceptual Styles

Dunn and Dunn (1993) also describe four perceptual styles that indicate a preference to learn new material by listening (auditory), by reading or viewing (visual), by touching (tactile), or by doing (kinesthetic). Auditory learners can easily remember things that they have heard and can reconstruct information that has been learned verbally. Visual learners prefer to read new material or view pictures or graphs. Taking notes or using their hands during the learning process is helpful to tactile learners. Kinesthetic learners benefit from the opportunity to participate actively in learning activities that allow movement and active practice.

Application to Workshops

Something for Everyone

Sociological Preferences. Designing a workshop by combining the something-for-everyone strategy with Dunn and Dunn's (1993) sociological preferences will result in the inclusion of activities that allow working alone, sharing in pairs, and interacting in groups. A workshop that allows only silent writing in response to reflection questions would not appeal to those learners who thrive on group interaction. Conversely, if every workshop activity requires large-group interaction, the needs of those who prefer to learn alone will not be met. To address each of these needs in a reflecting activity, you might start by asking participants to write their responses to questions on paper first, then have them share their answers with one other participant, and conclude by having the large group generate themes that emerged from the reflecting and sharing.

Another sociological aspect of workshop learning is whether participants prefer to learn from an authority figure or from peers. Lectures and other didactic presentations of information are likely to appeal to learners who prefer learning from authority figures. Participants who prefer to learn from peers will enjoy activities like structured discussions, simulations, and role-plays. A workshop that balances these two preferences will provide some learning activities that emphasize learning from the facilitator and other activities that emphasize peer learning.

➤ *What sociological preferences impact your own learning style? Do you prefer to learn alone, in pairs, in small groups, or in large groups? Do you prefer to learn from an authority or from peers?*

➤ *As a workshop facilitator, which sociological factors do you tend to emphasize? To provide more balance in the future, on which factors should you try to increase your emphasis?*

Perceptual Styles. The something-for-everyone strategy can also be combined with Dunn and Dunn's concept of perceptual styles by designing workshops that provide learning activities that correspond to each of these preferences. Auditory learners will be able to remember material that is presented verbally and will enjoy lectures, discussions, read-arounds, and storytelling. Visual learners will appreciate the opportunity to read handouts, view overheads, or participate in gallery exercises or map making. Tactile learners will benefit from the opportunity to take notes and are likely to find worksheets, card sorting, or artwork appealing. Kinesthetic learners enjoy participating in active learning and will respond positively to activities like practice role-plays, movement/sorting exercises, and psychodramas.

A workshop that is designed to appeal to all four perceptual styles can include activities that meet each of these needs. For example, a gardening workshop might start with a verbal description of useful techniques to meet the needs of auditory learners, then demonstrate the technique and provide a handout for visual learners, offer an opportunity for tactile learners to practice with plants and soil provided by the facilitator, and conclude with a tour of a community garden to allow the kinesthetic learners to move while learning. Examples of workshop activities that correspond to different perceptual styles also are summarized in Exhibit 2.1.

EXHIBIT 2.1
Activities That Correspond to Dunn and Dunn's Perceptual Styles

Auditory	*Visual*
Lecture	Handouts
Discussion	Overheads
Music	Gallery Exercises
Read-Arounds	Maps
Storytelling	Time Lines

Tactile	*Kinesthetic*
Worksheets	Movement/Sorting
Card Sorting	Practice Role-Plays
Artwork	Psychodrama

NOTE: Descriptions and examples of these activities are provided in Chapter 5.

➤ *What are your preferred perceptual styles? As a facilitator, which perceptual styles do your learning activities tend to match? What activities that match other perceptual styles could you use to create more holistic and balanced workshops?*

Measure and Match

To combine the measure-and-match strategy with Dunn and Dunn's model of learning styles, you can measure participants' needs using the Productivity Environmental Preference Survey (PEPS; Dunn, Dunn, & Price, 1986), which is an adult adaptation of Dunn, Dunn, and Price's (1989) Learning Styles Inventory. The PEPS consists of 100 items that measure learning preferences along 20 different dimensions, including sociological variables like the preference for learning from peers versus an authority figure, and perceptual styles that identify scores for auditory, visual, tactile, and kinesthetic learning. Sample items include, "The things I remember best are the things that I see or read," and "If I can go through each step of a task, I usually remember what I learned." It takes most adults 20 to 30 minutes to complete the PEPS. Unfortunately, the PEPS cannot be self-scored; a computer program can be purchased to administer the

PEPS, or answer sheets can be mailed in for scoring. Because of the cost of computer scoring or the time involved to mail surveys, use of PEPS with workshops is limited and is probably only cost- or time-efficient for use with a long-term training group rather than single-session workshops. If you do use the PEPS, it will allow you to identify sociological, perceptual, and other preferences within your group that you can use to select appropriate learning activities during workshop design.

➤ *As you think about the workshops you may present, are there groups for which it would be particularly helpful to use the Productivity Environmental Preference Survey as a part of needs assessment?*

Jung's Model of Psychological Type

Theory

One of the earliest models of individual differences that has implications for learning was described by Carl Jung (1971a) in his book *Psychological Types*. In describing how people's personalities differ from one another, Jung first made a fundamental distinction between two attitudes that he called extroversion and introversion. He described extroversion as "characterized by interest in the external object, responsiveness, and a ready acceptance of external happenings" (Jung, 1971b, p. 549). In contrast, he described introversion in this way: "Self-communings are a pleasure. His own world is a safe harbour. . . . His own company is the best" (Jung, 1971b, p. 551). In addition to these two attitudes, Jung distinguished between four functions—thinking, feeling, sensation, and intuition—that he described in this way: "The essential function of sensation is to establish that something exists, thinking tells us what it means, feeling what its value is, and intuition surmises whence it comes and whither it goes" (Jung, 1971b, p. 553).

Decades later, Jung's model was operationalized by the development of the Myers-Briggs Type Indicator (MBTI; Briggs & Myers, 1988). The MBTI contains four separate indices that measure the three preferences that Jung (1971a) identified and a fourth preference that was implied by Jung. First, the MBTI measures a preference for either extroversion or introversion. People with a preference for extroversion relate more easily to the outer world of people and things, whereas those with a preference for

EXHIBIT 2.2
Activities That Correspond to Extroversion and Introversion

Extroversion	*Introversion*
Icebreakers	Gallery Exercises
Brainstorming	Questionnaires/Instruments
Games and Simulations	Handouts
Read-Arounds	Worksheets
Practice Role-Plays	
Discussions	
Psychodrama	
Speak-Outs	

NOTE: Descriptions and examples of these activities are provided in Chapter 5.

introversion have interests in the inner world of concepts and ideas. Second, the MBTI measures whether individuals' perceptions are attuned to sensing or intuition. A preference for sensing is associated with working with known facts, reliance on direct information from the five senses, and a focus on immediate awareness. In contrast, a preference for intuition indicates a greater focus on possibilities, meanings, and relationships by way of insight. Third, the MBTI measures a distinction between thinking and feeling that indicates how people prefer to make decisions. Individuals with a preference for thinking make decisions based on logical analysis, whereas those with a preference for feeling make decisions based on personal values. Lastly, the MBTI measures the distinction between judging and perceiving, which describes how people orient themselves to the outer world. Individuals with a preference for judging like a planned, decided, orderly way of life and, in contrast, individuals with a preference for perceiving like a flexible, spontaneous way of life (Briggs & Myers, 1988).

Application to Workshops

Something for Everyone

Extroversion-Introversion. Combining the something-for-everyone strategy with Jung's model of psychological type involves designing a

EXHIBIT 2.3
Activities That Correspond to Sensing and Intuition

Sensing	Intuition
Case Studies	Storytelling
Questionnaires	Guided Fantasies
Time Lines	Brainstorming
Gallery Exercises	Scenarios
Maps	Goal Setting
	Action Plans

NOTE: Descriptions and examples of these activities are provided in Chapter 5.

workshop with learning activities that balance the needs of those with different preferences on each continuum. For example, to meet the needs of both introverts and extroverts, it will be important to provide opportunities to learn alone and to learn through interaction with others. Extroverts will prefer more interaction and will tend to enjoy activities like brainstorming, games, role-plays, and speak-outs. Workshop participants with a preference for introversion are more likely to enjoy less interactive activities that allow private responses to new ideas and concepts like gallery exercises, questionnaires, and handouts. A balanced workshop will provide some activities for extroverts and others for introverts. To balance your experimenting activities in this way you might want to provide a worksheet before proceeding to a practice role-play. Examples of learning activities that correspond to preferences for extroversion and introversion also are listed in Exhibit 2.2.

➤ *What can you do to make sure your workshops meet the needs of extroverted participants? How can you also respond to the needs of introverted participants?*

Sensing-Intuition. To design a workshop that balances preferences for sensing and intuition, you can provide opportunities to look at concrete facts and receive sensory input as well as allow for the consideration of future possibilities. Learners with a preference for sensing might be particularly drawn to activities that focus on the present experience or look at

EXHIBIT 2.4
Activities That Correspond to Thinking and Feeling

Thinking	Feeling
Lectures	Values Clarification
Group Surveys	Guided Fantasies
Questionnaires	Music
Case Studies	Movement/Sorting
Handouts	Practice Role-Plays
Maps	Artwork
Time Lines	

NOTE: Descriptions and examples of these activities are provided in Chapter 5.

concrete data like case studies, questionnaires, and time lines. Learning activities that correspond to a preference for intuition are more likely to look at patterns and possibilities and to look toward the future. Intuitive activities include brainstorming, guided fantasies, and action plans. A research methodology workshop designed to correspond to both sensing and intuition preferences might spend time examining research reports and analyzing methodological strengths and weaknesses (sensing) as well as generating a list of ideas for future research projects (intuition). Examples of learning activities that correspond to preferences for sensing and intuition also are listed in Exhibit 2.3.

➤ *As a workshop facilitator, what kinds of activities would you like to include to meet the needs of sensing participants? Which activities would you like to use to meet the needs of intuitive participants?*

Thinking-Feeling. To offer something for both participants with a preference for thinking and a preference for feeling, you can design activities that allow for logical analysis as well as the integration of personal values. Thinking activities encourage logical analysis and include lectures, surveys, questionnaires, and case studies. Feeling activities allow for the identification of personal values and include guided fantasies, values clarification, and practice role-plays. To balance thinking and feeling, a career planning workshop might include an opportunity for participants to construct a time line identifying critical incidents in their career development (thinking) as well as a guided fantasy that helps them imagine a typical work day 10 years in the future (feeling). Examples of learning activities that correspond to preferences for thinking or for feeling also are listed in Exhibit 2.4.

➤ *What can you do to make sure your workshops meet the needs of participants with a preference for thinking? How can you also appeal to those with a preference for feeling?*

Judging-Perceiving. In order to meet the needs of those with a preference for judging or for perceiving, a workshop can include a balance between structure and flexibility. Judging activities are those that offer more structure and linear order, like lectures. Perceiving activities are less structured and allow for more flexibility or spontaneity as would occur in an open discussion. It is more difficult for us to identify specific learning activities that correspond to a preference for judging or for perceiving. However, you can design and present most activities so that they are more structured and organized or in a way that allows more spontaneity and flexibility. To provide a balanced workshop that will appeal to participants with either preference, it may be best to structure some activities in a more orderly way and allow more flexibility in others.

➤ *What can you do as a workshop facilitator to provide a balance between orderly structure and flexible spontaneity?*

Measure and Match

In order to combine the measure-and-match strategy with Jung's model of psychological type, you can give the MBTI to participants before a workshop and use the results to customize the workshop to the personalities represented in the group. The potential to use the MBTI as a part of needs assessment is recognized in the MBTI manual, which identifies the test as a way "to develop different teaching methods to meet the needs of different types" and "to analyze curricula, methods, media, and materials in light of the needs of different types" (Myers & McCaulley, 1985, p. 4). The MBTI (Form G) contains 126 items and takes approximately 30 minutes to complete. The items present respondents with pairs of either words or phrases from which they must choose. The test scores result in scores on each of the four continua. Sample MBTI items include, "When you go somewhere for the day, would you rather (a) plan what you will do and when, or (b) just go?" and "When you are with a group of people, would you usually rather (a) join in the talk of the group, or (b) talk with one person at a time." When preferences on the four MBTI indices are combined, 16 unique psychological types can be identified.

Knowledge of participants' personalities can be used to choose activities that will meet the needs of diverse learners. For example, it might be appropriate to use the MBTI for needs assessment in a management workshop where you plan activities to highlight stylistic differences measured before the workshop. Some activities could be designed to point out the common characteristics of certain personalities by grouping managers with similar types. Other activities might emphasize the need to take different styles into consideration by grouping diverse managers together and having them complete tasks that will highlight the impact of their different styles.

➤ *As you think about the workshops you may present in the future, are there groups for which it would be particularly helpful to use the Myers-Briggs Type Indicator as a part of needs assessment?*

Other Factors That Impact Workshop Learning

Gender

Gender may also play a role in how participants learn in workshops. Both research studies (e.g., Belenky, Clinchy, Goldberger, & Tarule, 1986; DeFrancisco, 1992) and the popular press (e.g., Schaef, 1985; Tannen, 1994) have documented the differences between men and women and how these differences may affect learning and communication. Not all research shows gender differences in learning. However, the fact that many people perceive that there are gender differences in learning may be more relevant to workshop facilitation than are actual research findings. This perception may be further heightened by the topics of certain workshops, such as sexual harassment, sexual assault prevention, and assertiveness. Therefore, it is important that facilitators attend to the gender differences within the participant group, as well as between the group and the facilitator, and consider how these differences may affect workshop learning and participation (Sork,

1997). For instance, in a workshop about sexual harassment, you might want to consider using an activity like a fishbowl discussion (see Chapter 5), which allows men and women to learn from each other within the safety of their own gender group. On gender-sensitive topics with a mixed-gender group, it may be helpful for female and male cofacilitators to work together to model open dialogue and cooperation between men and women.

➤ *How do you think gender differences might impact the workshops that you are likely to present? Are there topics or activities that you present that might impact men and women differently? What can you do to ensure that your workshops meet the needs of both women and men?*

Culture

In addition to considering learning styles and gender, it also is necessary to take into account cultural background and other aspects of identity that may impact workshop learning. Sork (1997) encouraged workshop designers to consider multiple forms of diversity including gender, race, ethnicity, class, sexual orientation, linguistic background, religious orientation, and ability or disability. Although cultural identity may impact workshop learning in many ways, one of the most pervasive is the power dynamic that may result if there are gender or cultural differences between the facilitator and participants (Johnson-Bailey & Cervero, 1997). Although you should learn about the cultural composition of your workshop group and consider how culture may impact communication, participation, regard for facilitators, and patterns of relating to other groups, it is dangerous to rely on generalizations or stereotypes and overlook individual differences within groups (Sork, 1997). Some significant cultural differences related to workshop learning include comfort with self-disclosure; attitudes toward authority figures; and types of activities preferred, such as auditory versus visual learning or group versus individual work (e.g., Jalali, 1988; Kraemer, 1996; Sork, 1997; Vasquez, 1990).

Wlodkowski (1997) presented a model of culturally responsive teaching that recognized that motivation is inseparable from culture. This model stressed the necessity of nurturing intrinsic motivation in workshop participants rather than depending on culturally determined extrinsic rewards such as grades or status. Wlodkowski suggested that cultivating intrinsic motivation involves establishing inclusion, developing a favorable attitude toward learning, enhancing meaning, and engendering competence. Addressing these aspects of motivation in a culturally sensitive manner creates a climate that welcomes and accommodates diverse workshop learners. Asking participants to identify what they want to learn from the workshop and reinforcing the idea of intrinsic motivation may be a way to create a welcoming climate. Because of the importance of addressing culture and other issues of diversity in workshops, we have emphasized diversity-based examples throughout the book.

➤ *What kinds of cultural or other differences are likely to be present in your workshops? What can you do to meet the needs of participants from different backgrounds?*

Summary

This chapter introduced two strategies for workshop design called Something for Everyone and Measure and Match. Each of these strategies was applied to three different models of individual differences likely to impact workshop learning. Ideas for how to create a balanced workshop using activities that meet the needs of different participants were presented, followed by ideas about how to use different instruments in needs assessment to customize a workshop design for a specific group. The chapter concluded by briefly considering gender and cultural differences that may impact workshop learning.

Planning for Application

1. List the most prominent individual differences that you think are present in the workshops that you regularly facilitate or might facilitate in the future.

2. With these differences in mind, how might you modify your workshops to respond better to these differences?

Chapter

3

Preparing for Workshop Design

Gathering Information and Setting Goals

Consider the last time you went on a vacation or business trip. What kind of information did you gather to prepare for your trip? How did you decide when and where to go? What kind of plans did you make to ensure a pleasurable trip? What kind of information did you collect about your destination? How did you decide what to pack and where to stay? What were your most important goals for the trip?

Designing a workshop may be like setting up your exact travel itinerary and deciding what to do each day. However, a great deal of information must be collected and preliminary decisions must be made before an itinerary can be definitively set. Five separate tasks in this preparation process are explored in this chapter. First, collecting preliminary workshop information; second, making decisions about whether the workshop should be presented and the resulting formal or informal agreement; third, assessing or predicting the learning needs of workshop participants; fourth, using this information to set workshop goals and learning objectives; and last, identifying material resources that can be used to enhance workshop learning.

Reflecting on Preparation

Before we suggest specific ways for you to prepare for workshop design, we would like you to think about how you have prepared for past workshops or other presentations.

1. What kind of information do you usually collect before you begin to plan a workshop or presentation? Were there times when you failed to collect information that you later realized was important?

---

2. Have you ever conducted a formal needs assessment with participants before designing a learning experience? If so, how did you assess these needs? If not, what information did you rely on to anticipate participants' learning needs?

---

3. What kinds of goals and objectives do you tend to emphasize in your workshops?

Preparation Time and Effort

The time and effort it takes to prepare for workshop design varies widely. For a short workshop on a familiar topic with a known audience, you may only take a few minutes to gather information, and goal setting may be an implicit process as you plunge directly into designing the workshop. On the other hand, for a longer workshop with an unknown or important audience, or with a new topic, you may want to collect much more information about the participants and set goals and make arrangements in greater detail. For example, one of us recently presented a workshop on an unfamiliar topic to a university president and 20 top administrators. This was somewhat intimidating and preparation started months before the workshop. In contrast to this experience, each of us also has been asked to do workshops on more familiar ground in which we might spend only a few minutes collecting information before moving on to the design.

Gathering Preliminary Information

There are several key questions that need to be answered before you decide to present a particular workshop to a particular group. We have identified eight important areas to consider and organized them around the journalist's questions of who, what, why, when, where, and how. These questions are summarized in Exhibit 3.1.

Who Is Initiating This Workshop?

Some workshops are initiated by the facilitator and some are requested by others. If you are initiating a workshop that you intend to facilitate, you will have to make decisions about the topic, content, and purpose. If someone else is requesting the workshop, they already will have ideas about the topic and purpose, and you will consult with them and negotiate these decisions. Although, in some instances, you may be playing both the role of initiator and designer/facilitator, the following sections are written with the assumption that these are separate roles.

What Is the Relationship Between the Requester and the Participants?

Is the requester an equal member of the group who will be participating or is he or she a leader, supervisor, or instructor? If the requester is a leader rather than a member of the group, do the potential participants agree with the requester about the need for the workshop? Will this leader actually be attending the workshop? In some settings, more genuine learning may take place if the leader or requester is absent. Without an authority figure present, participants may feel freer to express divergent opinions, discuss controversial issues, or develop creative solutions to long-standing problems. On the other hand, there are other situations when it is important for the requester to attend to maintain accountability and/or respect for the facilitator. For example, one of us presented a workshop requested by a university resident advisor to deal with problems on her floor. Shortly

EXHIBIT 3.1
Key Questions in Gathering Preliminary Information

Who?	Who is initiating the workshop?
	Who will be attending the workshop?
What?	What are the topic, title, and content of the workshop?
Why?	Why is the workshop being requested or offered?
When?	When will the workshop be offered?
	How long will the workshop last?
Where?	Where will the workshop take place?
How?	What arrangements will be made? By whom?

before the workshop, the advisor said she would be leaving halfway through the allotted time. As soon as this "authority figure" left, the workshop descended into near chaos and participants offered challenges at every turn. It is hoped that this workshop would have gone more smoothly if the facilitator had been supported by an ally with whom the participants had an ongoing relationship. Therefore, it is important to consider the impact that the presence or absence of a leader may have on your workshop group.

What Is the Relationship Between
the Requester and the Facilitator?

How do you know the requester? On the basis of what knowledge is the requester asking you to present this workshop? The relationship between the requester and facilitator typically is one of the following: (a) The facilitator is part of the same organization, office, or unit; or (b) the facilitator is an outside consultant or guest speaker. If you are a member of the same organization, then your workshop may be part of your regular responsibilities. If you are an outside consultant, it will be important to gather more information and negotiate a fee or another type of reward for the work you will be doing.

Who Else Is Invested in the Workshop?

A relatively new concept in the business world is that of "worker as learner" (Onstenk, 1995). Onstenk (1992) describes this as a shift from the traditional perspective where the company thinks for the worker to wanting the worker to think for the company. This desire to capitalize on individual thought and creativity requires employers to encourage ongoing professional development and to value the learning process. This is a positive development for those of us who do workshops, because it may mean that we will be invited more often into corporate and professional settings in addition to more traditional academic and social service settings. However, this new group of requesters may have different expectations of us in terms of compensation, content, and, especially, effectiveness. It is essential to assess these expectations early and to factor them into the resulting workshop agreement. In addition, in the business world, the results of the workshop may be related to "higher stakes," such as decisions to invite you back, continue the training program, or continue to fund worker development programs.

Sork (1997) highlighted the need to ask, "Whose interests are being served by the workshop?" This introduces the important issue of other *stakeholders* who have a stake or interest in the workshop and therefore should be involved in workshop planning. Workshops are rarely offered at only the participants' request. Usually there are additional stakeholders in the workshop process and outcome, such as the supervisor who wants her employees to learn a new skill, the resident advisor who needs to present a workshop as part of his contract, or the company that wants to introduce managers to a particular method of conflict management. All of these individuals should be a part of the information-gathering and goal-setting process.

Who Will Be Attending the Workshop?

How many participants are expected to attend? Are the participants members of an intact group with ongoing contact such as a work group, a class, or a community organization? If the group is intact, you will be working not only with a group of individuals, but also with a functioning "social system" (Stech & Ratcliffe, 1977). Is the workshop openly advertised and likely to attract participants who do not know one another? What are the expectations of the participants for the workshop in terms of formality, content, helpfulness, and so on? It also may be helpful to know whether attendance is required of any or all of the participants. Knowledge of all of these factors will help you anticipate group dynamics that will impact workshop learning.

What Is the Relationship Between the
Facilitator and the Participants?

Do you know some or all of the participants? Will you relate to them as an expert or as a peer? As an outsider or as a colleague? If you know the participants, you will be more familiar with the particular needs or group dynamics. On the other hand, if you are familiar to the participants in a way that is not conducive to a leadership or facilitator role, it may be necessary to establish a different pattern of relating at the onset of the workshop. Your prior relationship to workshop participants may determine what type of role you choose as a facilitator. The role of facilitator differs according to factors such as formality, authority, and credibility.

What Are the Topic, Title, and Content of the Workshop?

Topic

The requester of the workshop will probably have an idea of the topic, but sometimes you will merely be presented with an idea or a problem and you may be asked to suggest a topic that would address the idea or solve the problem. Sometimes requesters have an idea that may be unrealistic or outside your area of expertise. You may need to say, "I can't do a workshop on X, but I do know a lot more about Y or Z, which may provide a slightly different approach to the same issue. Do you think that would meet the needs of your group?"

Title

The importance of the title varies according to the situation. If the workshop will be presented to an intact group with participants who are required or highly motivated to attend, then the title need only be informative and descriptive of the content. However, if the workshop is open and advertised, the title must have marketing appeal and catch the attention of potential participants, in addition to being accurate. At the time of gathering preliminary information, you and the requester need to agree upon a title that is accurate and informative as well as catchy and provocative. One common strategy is to choose a title that provokes an image and then add a descriptive phrase as a subtitle. For example: "Life in the fast lane: Strategies to avoid burnout"; "Just say no!: Avoiding overcommitment at work and home"; "Breaking up is hard to do: Surviving the loss of a romantic relationship."

Content

You also must decide what content should be covered. The amount and depth of coverage will be determined, in part, by the allocated time and the background knowledge and experience of the participants. You will want to get some initial ideas from the requester but also make decisions or changes of your own as you progress farther into the design. If major changes in content seem to be appropriate after an initial agreement has been made, you will need to inform the requester and get his or her input or approval.

Why Is the Workshop Being Requested or Offered?

What is the purpose of the workshop? As stated in Chapter 1, workshops are usually offered for one of several reasons: (a) to solve a problem, (b) to teach new skills, (c) to provide new information, (d) to change a system, or (e) to increase awareness and promote self-improvement. The purpose the workshop is designed to serve will influence the motivation of the participants and their openness or resistance to new learning

When Will the Workshop Be Offered?

Do you have enough time to prepare? Your preparation time will vary according to your background and the complexity of the workshop content. There are workshops that each of us have presented before that we could do tomorrow. Other topics might take us weeks to prepare. The number of days or weeks you need to prepare also depends on how busy you are during that time. Can you set aside the time you need to prepare before the date set for the workshop?

How Long Will the Workshop Last?

Is there enough time to cover the topic adequately? Requesters often ask facilitators to do too much in too little time. This leads to problems, including an overreliance on didactic material to the neglect of experiential learning. If you believe that you can't do a good job in the time requested, you have a choice to make. You can ask for more time or you can agree to do less. With the limited time that most workshop facilitators face, they must set limits and focus in greater depth on the most essential knowledge or skills. It is better to do less and do it well than to do too much and do it poorly. You may need to negotiate with the requester: "In that amount of time, I don't think I can cover all three of those topics. Of the three, which set of skills is it most important for these participants to learn?"

Where Will the Workshop Take Place?

Is This a Suitable Physical Environment?

If you are designing an experiential workshop that encourages activity or movement, then you need to ensure that the room or space is large enough to accommodate the type of activities that you would like to use. The size of the room may limit the number of participants who can attend. Other environmental concerns include seating arrangements and tables. Can you rearrange the room if necessary? Do the participants need tables on which to write? (See Chapter 6 for a further discussion of the workshop learning environment.)

Whose Turf Is This?

Where the workshop takes place may impact the mood by suggesting it is the "turf" or "home territory" of either the facilitator or the participants. Are the participants coming to your turf or are you going to theirs? There are advantages to both arrangements. Your own turf suggests your authority, whereas the participants' turf suggests your availability. Neutral turf outside the work environment may be more conducive to new creative solutions that may not be fostered within the everyday workplace.

What Arrangements Will Be Made? By Whom?

What arrangements will be made by the requester? What arrangements will the facilitator need to take care of? What materials will be provided? What equipment should be arranged for? What other resources are needed? Who will make these arrangements? Morrisey, Sechrest, and Warman (1997) refer to this category of information as "logistics," and strongly encourage facilitators to be active in making these arrangements. They remind us that, although it might not feel like "our job," for instance, to make sure that the heat is on, it certainly will be our problem if it is not.

➤ *When you think about the workshops that you will present in the future, are there other types of information that you think you should collect?*

Negotiating a Workshop Agreement

All of the elements of preliminary information should be discussed or explored before you agree or decide to facilitate a workshop. Vaught, Hoy, and Buchanan (1985) call this the "decision stage" and note the multiple levels of decisions that are needed to finalize a workshop decision: Who will initiate, design and structure, administer, select participants, evaluate, and who will be held accountable?

As may be obvious by now, in most cases workshop facilitators need to function as consultants before they can become presenters. In other words, facilitators need to spend time with the requesters, assessing their expectations and participant needs before it can even be determined that a workshop is the appropriate intervention for a particular group. Thinking of yourself initially as a consultant may help you slow down and collect the information you need, rather than feeling pressed to agree to provide a workshop.

At this point, you also must consider your motivation for doing the workshop. If you are facilitating this workshop for a fee, this too must be negotiated before you formally agree. Is the fee you are going to be paid sufficient for the amount of work it will take to prepare for and present the workshop? If you are not being paid for the workshop, are there other incentives that you should consider? Besides being paid a fee for services, other incentives include facilitating as part of your regular job, helping another unit within your organization, contributing to your own professional development, creating publicity for a related endeavor that may result in more business, adding to your own professional status or reputation, doing a favor for a colleague, or contributing to your community. It is helpful to identify the incentives and your motivation for providing the workshop as a way of measuring the cost and benefit to yourself for the time and effort involved in preparing for and presenting a workshop.

Here are some questions to ask yourself before deciding whether to present a workshop (or whether you should initiate one yourself):

Am I the best person to facilitate this workshop?
Do I have enough background knowledge? If not, can I collect it?
Can I design an effective intervention for these participants?
Are my facilitation skills appropriate for these participants?
Should I involve a cofacilitator?
Do I have enough time to prepare?
What are the expectations of the requester? Of the participants? Of other
    stakeholders?
Is the fee or the other incentives sufficient for the work involved?
What are the consequences of the potential results of this workshop? For
    instance, are there "high stakes" issues such as the continuation of a training
    program involved?

Depending upon your situation and the relationship between you and the
requester, the formality of the workshop agreement can range from a casual
phone call to a written contract. At a minimum, the workshop agreement
should cover the elements summarized in Exhibit 3.2.

➤ *What are some of the topics you are well prepared to present? What are some*
workshop topics that you would be willing to present only if you had sufficient time
to expand your knowledge? What are some workshop topics that, if requested,
you would decline to present? Why? What fees would you charge for a workshop?
If you don't charge fees, what other benefits would you expect to receive to
compensate you for your time and energy?

Determining the Needs of Workshop Participants

One of the most important reasons for gathering information before designing a workshop is to determine the learning needs of the workshop participants. These needs form the basis for goal setting and workshop design. As
stated by Dipboye (1997), "a properly conducted needs assessment identifies the focus of the training" (p. 33). Traditionally, many approaches to
adult education have stressed the importance of extensive needs assessment
based on surveys or interviews with participants before the workshop. For
some situations this sort of assessment is helpful; however, this ideal is
often impractical or unnecessary. For many workshops, participants cannot
be identified ahead of time; in other situations the time and energy needed
for formal needs assessment are not available. In many situations, the

EXHIBIT 3.2
Minimum Elements in a Workshop Agreement

Workshop Title
Basic Content
Date, Time, and Length of Workshop
Fee/Incentives
Responsibilities of Both Parties
Arrangements
Materials
Publicity

---

learning needs of participants can be predicted based on prior experience of the facilitator or requester or can be determined within the workshop itself. Therefore, in this section of the chapter, we discuss formal needs assessment as one of four strategies for determining the needs of workshop participants; also included are needs prediction, assessment within workshops, and customizing learning to the needs of a workshop group. We also discuss assessing the needs or desires of the requester and other stakeholders.

Before spending the time and effort to conduct a formal needs assessment, determine whether one is actually necessary. Generally, the length of the workshop, your access to the participants ahead of time, and the depth of the material are indicators of the necessity and feasibility of the assessment. Consider the following questions:

Can I predict the needs of the participants without a formal assessment?
Do I know, specifically, who will be coming to the workshop?
Am I familiar with the general characteristics of the participants?
Can the requester provide me with sufficient information about the participants?

Formal Needs Assessment

The hallmark of formal needs assessment is collecting information directly from participants before you design the workshop and basing the design on this information. Formal needs assessment information can be collected in several ways (for more complete discussions of needs assessment techniques, see sources such as Soriano, 1995, and Witkin & Altschuld, 1995). First, you can ask participants to fill out a written survey or questionnaire before the workshop (e.g., Bertcher, 1988, pp. 58-68; Soriano, 1995, pp. 50-63; Witkin & Altschuld, 1995, pp. 131-145). Typically, the questions might address knowledge, attitudes, or motivation related to the workshop content. You can then use this information to tailor the workshop to the unique needs of the group. For example, through surveying the background knowledge of a group, you might learn that there are some people who know a lot more about the subject matter than others. On the basis of this information, you might choose to spend part of the workshop with the participants divided into two different groups so that the material can be addressed at both a basic and a more advanced level.

The second way to assess the needs of a workshop group is to interview the participants before the workshop (e.g., Bertcher, 1988, pp. 58-68; Morrisey et al., 1997, p. 21). This approach is especially helpful when the purpose of the workshop is systemic change within an organization. If you are trying to improve the relationships within an intact work group, it may be particularly important to get an idea of the group dynamics and personality conflicts that contribute to the problem. It is much easier to gather this type of complex information from interviews than from written materials.

A third way to assess the needs of the group directly is to review written materials such as work samples or supervisor evaluations (e.g., Soriano, 1995, pp. 16-19; Witkin & Altschuld, 1995, pp. 109-119). Alternately, you can interview supervisors regarding the learning needs of their supervisees. If this type of material is reviewed, you can get direct insight into the needs of the participants. For example, if you are doing a workshop on report writing, it may be helpful to review materials that workshop participants have written in the past so that you can gear your teaching toward areas of weakness. On the other hand, if you are doing a workshop related to improving work productivity, it may be helpful to read supervisors' ratings of employees so that your workshop can address the kind of issues with which the participants actually struggle.

Additional, perhaps more nontraditional, ways of engaging in needs assessment might include calling potential participants and asking about their top concerns and needs, acquiring newsletters or annual reports published by the requesting department or group, or looking over relevant publicity or publications about the industry or profession in question (D'Arcy, 1992). You also may be able to talk with someone who has previously facilitated a workshop with that participant group (Morrisey et al., 1997).

To assist in participant assessments that occur before a workshop, you may want to devise a worksheet that helps you remember the types of information you want to gather. For instance, Lambert (1988) advocates an "audience research checklist" (p. 10) in which items such as, "The primary reason the audience is attending" and "How familiar do you expect the average person . . . to be with your topic?" are listed. Another worksheet example is offered in D'Arcy (1992, pp. 56-57) and features sections such as "situation" and "audience." These types of lists or worksheets can ensure you get the information you need to best design the workshop. If you are a person for whom worksheets are helpful, we encourage you to develop your own using the ideas presented above or in the sources we cited.

Needs Prediction

Even if you do not conduct a formal needs assessment, it is necessary to predict the needs of participants. Some of the preliminary information collected before agreeing to present the workshop will form the basis for this prediction. In addition, you will consider the needs of the participants related to knowledge, attitudes, and motivation. In most cases, you will want to predict the needs of participants based on either your own past experience or information that you gather from the requester.

Assessment Within Workshops

In many cases, it is possible or even preferable to assess needs within the workshop. Several learning activities can be used to serve the dual purposes of assessing the knowledge or attitudes of the participants as well as to promote experiential learning within the workshop. For example, questionnaires, surveys, and sorting exercises (see Chapter 5) are all learning activities that allow you to assess needs within a workshop. By including these activities at the beginning of a workshop, you will facilitate learning about the group as well as collect valuable information that can be used to tailor subsequent activities more accurately to the unique needs of a particular group.

The simplest form of assessing needs within a workshop is to ask participants to tell you what they would like to learn. If you do this, you need enough time and flexibility to be responsive to these expressed needs. Of course, it may not be possible to meet all the desires that are shared, and it is best to clarify which needs you will and will not be able to address in the time and format allotted. Assessing needs within a workshop allows a greater degree of spontaneity and flexibility than a traditional needs assessment that takes place before the workshop.

A common thread among these types of informal needs assessments is simply using your own background knowledge and common sense. Utilize your past experiences as a workshop presenter and requester to inform your planning. After all, you are the expert who was asked to facilitate the workshop—make sure you are using that expertise!

Determining the Needs of the Requester and Other Stakeholders

We want to reemphasize the importance of talking with the group leader or supervisor and other stakeholders. It is crucial to assess the expectations and outcomes desired by all involved. For instance, if you have been invited to facilitate a training session for a large company, it may make sense to talk to the requester's supervisor as well as the requester, to get a sense of what the company as a whole wants. Discover where the initial idea for having a training session came from and talk with that person. The requester may have misinterpreted what the boss wanted to have the workshop accomplish. You, the requester, and the participants will be far better off if you are able to clarify this in the design stage of your workshop.

In addition to assessing the needs of participants, you will also want to assess the needs of the other stakeholders involved. Stakeholder needs may be similar to those of the participants, but may also differ. For instance, you may be asked to provide an effective communication workshop for middle managers at a large corporation. The managers learn to state their needs and disappointments effectively and assertively and begin to do so in the workplace. However, the president of the company perceives that a major result of your workshop is that her subordinates "complain" more, and she calls into question the usefulness of further training. You were hired to improve worker performance, but a result of your workshop is increased criticism of the very individual who hired you! Your ability to assess the varying needs, as well as predict the results of various types of intervention, will greatly aid your ability to communicate up front with all of the stakeholders. In addition, you will be able to identify more appropriate goals and learning objectives as well as create a workshop agreement that will meet the needs of all involved.

Customizing Learning to the Needs of a Group

With many workshop topics, you will be able to customize learning to the specific needs of participants. The key to customizing a workshop using the four quadrants of our design model is to use each quadrant as a way to prepare for the next quadrant. For example, collecting information during reflecting activities lays the groundwork for subsequent learning. Information about individual needs that participants share during reflection can be used as examples during assimilation. Reflecting on experience also can identify areas for experimenting. If skills or strategies are identified or taught during assimilation, then these can be applied to practical situations that were elicited in reflection. When you are planning for application, you can encourage participants to choose between strategies presented during assimilating that they will practice in their own lives after the workshop.

➤ *For the workshops that you anticipate presenting, would a formal needs assessment be necessary or helpful? Why or why not? If you do conduct a formal needs assessment, what methods will you use? What will you assess? If you choose not to conduct a formal needs assessment, how will you predict the needs of workshop participants? How will you assess the needs of the workshop requester and other stakeholders?*

What Kinds of Needs Should Be Determined?

Knowledge

What do participants already know about the topic you are presenting? What do they need to learn about the topic? Do all participants have about the same level of background knowledge? If not, it may be important to provide both introductory information and more advanced knowledge. An ideal way of solving this problem may be to spend part of the workshop in small groups that are divided according to knowledge or experience related to the topic. For example, professional staff and support staff within an office or organization may need to break into different groups to address the particular needs of these subgroups.

Attitudes

It is advisable to predict whether the participants in the workshop will generally be in agreement with what you have to say or not. Sometimes a group will be divided in attitudes, and it is usually more helpful to acknowledge rather than ignore these differences. There are learning activities that both acknowledge these subgroups and use this knowledge as an integral aspect of workshop learning. For example, sorting exercises are a helpful way to explicate within-group differences (see Chapter 5). Learning activities can be used to lead into a discussion such as, "Now that we have identified these different opinions, how can we use this information to help the group function without letting this disagreement interfere?"

If your attitudes or the position presented in the workshop differs from the opinions of the audience, you may want to begin the workshop by clarifying assumptions (see Chapters 6 and 7). If you begin by clarifying your assumptions, you can let the participants know where you are coming from and acknowledge differences from the outset. When you encounter attitudes with which you strongly disagree, it often is useful to use other participants to confront these attitudes. Your "expertise" may not be as persuasive as the similarity of the other participants. For example, you can "bounce" difficult questions back to the group (see Chapter 7). This will promote healthy disagreement and dialogue within the workshop environment.

Motivation

There are several factors related to motivation that can be informally predicted. First, is the workshop voluntary or mandatory? If the workshop is voluntary, then initial motivation should be at least moderately high. Your initial responsibility is to capture that motivation and increase it. One of the advantages of experiential learning is that it can maintain interest and motivation. If the workshop is mandatory, you need to spend some time "selling" the value of the workshop or customizing it to the needs of the participants. It is important to give the audience the opportunity to tell you what they want to learn and to bridge the gap between their expectations and what you realistically can offer. Encouraging participants to reflect on their own experience begins to bridge that gap. Working with what they bring is another important step.

For intact groups, like a work group or an ongoing class, it may be helpful to obtain information about group dynamics. Knowledge about both the overt structure, such as who supervises whom, as well as the covert structure about informal alliances and friendships, can inform your design. Workshops for intact groups are often requested because of perceived problems related to the topic area. If this is the case, it will be helpful to know some of the background and group dynamics related to the topic. For example, a workshop on sexual harassment may tend to divide the group along gender lines. A workshop on quality assurance may divide the participants between management and labor.

➤ *What kinds of knowledge, attitudes, or motivation should be determined before your next workshop? How will you determine these needs?*

Setting Goals and Learning Objectives

Goals

An extremely useful way to organize your thinking and prepare for designing a workshop is to set goals and objectives. Goals are broad aims or purposes that identify general domains where learning will occur. Goals can sometimes be identified by asking yourself, "Why am I facilitating a workshop on this topic to this group of participants at this time?" (D'Arcy, 1992).

Learning Objectives

Learning objectives are more specific and measurable methods of realizing goals. Learning objectives answer the questions, "How will the goals be met?" and "What will the participants actually learn?" Note that objectives focus on "What is the desired result?" rather than "What will I say?" (Morrisey et al., 1997). Ideally, learning objectives are positive, realistic, relevant, specific, measurable, and flexible.

Positive. "Workshop participants will learn different strategies to make better use of time," is preferred over, "Participants will stop making bad decisions about time."

Realistic. "You will learn to identify ways to use communication more effectively," is more realistic than, "Your ability to communicate on the job will increase dramatically overnight."

Relevant. "Participants will learn to recognize the ways they have been taught to think about other ethnic groups with inaccurate stereotypes," is probably more relevant to a diversity workshop than, "We will review the five-hundred-year history of imperialism and oppression in North America."

Specific. "We will be reviewing three different theories about conflict resolution. The three theories are . . . ," is more specific than, "We will talk about why people argue with each other."

Measurable. "As a result of this workshop, you will be able to identify three ways to improve your relationship through positive communication," is more measurable than, "Communication in your relationship will improve after the workshop."

Flexible. Learning objectives often need to bend a bit during the course of a workshop. Although we don't recommend radically changing the workshop plan, you may find yourself spending more time on some topics and less on others, or needing to introduce a topic more or less thoroughly than you had intended. Allow yourself to flex with and respond to the participants' immediate needs.

Content Versus Learning Process Objectives

Most workshop designers organize learning objectives around content by specifying the material that will be learned. The disadvantage of content-based objectives is that they tend to steer the workshop design toward the learning process of assimilating and conceptualizing and to neglect the other three experiential learning processes. An alternative that will help you enact our experiential workshop model is to organize objectives around learning processes. For example, here are some learning process objectives for a time management workshop:

Reflecting on Experience. "Participants will reflect on past experience and recognize their own strengths and weaknesses regarding time management."

Assimilating and Conceptualizing. "Participants will learn about three strategies for effective time management, and these strategies will be applied to participants' current time management styles. The first strategy is . . ."

Experimenting and Practicing. "Participants will gain hands-on experience setting priorities, completing a personal schedule, and identifying time wasters that can be eliminated."

Planning for Application. "Participants will identify areas where they can personally apply chosen strategies and will share their action plans with other participants."

➤ *What kinds of goals and objectives will you use in your next workshop?*

Choosing Additional Resources

Types of Resources

The most important resources in a workshop are you, the facilitator, and the group of learners. However, what you say and do can be enhanced by the use of additional resources. Most workshop resources fall into one of four categories:

Up-Front Displays such as a chalk or marker board, an overhead projector, or slide projector.
Written Materials such as handouts and worksheets.
Multimedia Resources such as music, videotapes, or computer-generated media.
Interactive Resources such as games, simulation materials, or interactive computer activities.

In the MTV/World Wide Web era, participants increasingly expect to be visually entertained while they learn. As you prepare for workshop design, it is important to consider how to impart information and promote interactive learning in a stimulating manner.

Using Resources to Promote Experiential Learning

Rather than reviewing the specific uses of different types of resources and media, we will address the ways that these resources can be used to promote the four experiential learning processes. First and foremost, it is important to make sure that visual aids are used to encourage active rather than passive learning. Using a video or other media should be a way to "kick start" experiential learning rather than a substitute for interaction. For example, have participants actively respond to video materials by answering stimulus questions about the video. In the same way, handouts can be made into worksheets so that they encourage reflection, experimentation, or application.

Reflecting on Experience

Media and other resources can be used to encourage reflection on experience in two different ways. First, the use of media such as music or a video can remind participants of an experience they have had in the past. Second, media can create a common experience that participants can reflect on together. As you are encouraging participants to reflect on experience, it also may be helpful for them to write down their reflections before they share them with other participants. Worksheets with stimulus questions like "When was the first time you learned about . . .?" encourage reflection.

Assimilating and Conceptualizing

When you are presenting new information to workshop participants and asking them to think about how it applies to their own lives, try to present the information in a visually interesting manner. Overheads, slides, videos, and handouts all enhance visual learning to complement what you say verbally. Computer programs like Microsoft Powerpoint can make it easier to design colorful, stimulating overheads and slides. Videos or computer-generated displays can be used to present visual information that cannot be presented on an overhead projector. With technical or visual information, it is wise to use media that do justice to the material you are presenting. Poorly prepared visuals can dilute or diminish what you are presenting verbally.

Experimenting and Practicing

To promote experimental and practical learning, use specific resources to match the conditions in a work or life situation as closely as possible. Games and simulations that have physical props may be particularly helpful. For example, if you are doing a health promotion workshop, you may want to let participants practice with medical or exercise equipment rather than just talking about it. If the workshop promotes the use of computers or other technology, then it is best to have computers available with which to experiment and practice.

Planning for Application

When you are helping participants plan for application, you can provide written worksheets that serve as action plans. Videos can also be used to demonstrate an application that encourages participants to plan for their own application after the workshop. Regardless of the resources you use, they should promote active planning that allows participants to commit to a specific course of action after the workshop.

➤ *What kinds of material resources do you hope to use in future workshops? How can you ensure that they promote active and interactive learning?*

Summary

This chapter has reviewed several steps in the process of preparing for workshop design. First, key questions related to preliminary information gathering were presented. Second, the decisions related to a workshop agreement were reviewed. Third, methods of predicting or assessing participants' needs were discussed. Fourth, setting goals and objectives was described as the culmination of the information-gathering process. Finally, the ways that additional resources can be used to promote experiential learning were highlighted. Once you, the workshop designer, have gathered information and set goals and objectives, you are ready for the process of workshop design, which is the subject of Chapters 4 and 5.

Planning for Application

Think about the next workshop you plan to present and answer the following questions:

1. What kind of information do you need to collect before you decide to present the workshop?

_____

2. What will you do to assess or predict the needs of your workshop participants?

_____

3. What kinds of goals and objectives will you set for the workshop?

_____

4. What kinds of physical resources will you use to enhance each of the following types of experiential learning?

    a. Reflecting on Experience

_____

    b. Assimilating and Conceptualizing

_____

    c. Experimenting and Practicing

_____

    d. Planning for Application

_____

Chapter

4

Creating a
Comprehensive
Workshop Design

In order to build a house and make it livable, two sequential processes are necessary. First, you construct the foundation, walls, and roof of the house. Second, you fill the house with furniture, appliances, and other day-to-day necessities. When you enter a newly constructed house, you can see the layout and floor plan—"here's the kitchen, this must be the master bedroom"—but most of us would not want to live in an empty house. To transform a house into a livable home, you will probably want to paint the walls, put up curtains, put a bed in the bedroom, some furniture in the living room, and probably a refrigerator with some food in the kitchen.

These two processes provide a useful metaphor for thinking about workshop design. Building the basic structure of a house is analogous to creating an overall workshop design. Decorating the individual rooms and filling them with furniture is similar to the process of designing specific workshop activities. Only after a general workshop framework has been created can the individual activities be fleshed out to fit the goals, objectives, and overall structure. Creating a comprehensive plan for your workshop is the topic of this chapter. Filling in this structure by designing individual learning activities is addressed in Chapter 5.

The steps that lead to a comprehensive workshop structure include choosing a consistent theme, planning ways to begin and end the workshop, providing different types of learning activities, arranging these activities in a meaningful sequence, and considering the overall length of the workshop. Each of these steps will be discussed sequentially. We conclude the chapter with a sample outline that illustrates many of the design considerations discussed.

Reflecting on Workshop Design

1. Can you think of a particularly well-designed workshop that you have presented or attended? What made this workshop appealing?

_____

2. Did this workshop weave a consistent theme through the different activities? How would you describe this theme?

_____

3. Did this workshop use a variety of learning activities to address the same topic? What kinds of activities were used?

_____

4. Can you think of a poorly designed workshop you have attended? What made this workshop less appealing?

_____

Choosing a Consistent Theme

In a successful workshop, different elements fit together to form a complete learning experience. One of the most effective ways to provide consistency throughout a workshop is to choose a theme that will guide your design and can be used to tie together different learning activities. The theme you choose should be based on your assessment of the group's needs and the goals and objectives you have set for the workshop. For example, a workshop on workplace communication might be guided by the theme, "Communication includes both the message that is sent and the message that is received. To communicate clearly, we must ensure that what we say is being heard without interference or distortion." A workshop on gender roles might be organized around the theme, "Men and women are each taught half of the skills needed by a fully functioning human," or "We have each been taught many gender lessons, some of which have been helpful to us and others that have limited our development."

The theme you select is likely to reflect one of the workshop emphases listed in Chapter 1. For example, you can use a theme to highlight an emphasis on skill building, problem solving, increasing knowledge, systemic change, or personal awareness and self-improvement. Once a workshop theme has been selected, it can be used to guide the selection and design "behind the scenes," or it can be announced to the participants and used as an overt signpost for organization of the workshop. In the latter case, the theme can be introduced at the beginning of the workshop and each activity related to it as a method of reinforcement and consistency. For longer workshops, you may want to select more than one theme, focusing on different aspects of the topic during various segments. For example, a full-day workshop may focus on one theme in the morning and a second in the afternoon. A multiday workshop could explore different themes each day.

➤ *Given the workshop topics that you are likely to present, can you identify themes you would like to emphasize? How can you use these themes to guide your workshop designs?*

Beginning and Ending Your Workshop

No matter how you choose to design your workshop, make sure that it has a beginning, a middle, and an end. Although this is a simple idea, both of us have participated in workshops that seemed to be just a string of activities that suddenly ended without warning. Most workshops should start with an introduction and overview that set the stage for the interactive learning that will take place. Likewise, your workshop should end with a conclusion that brings closure to the learning experience. The introduction and conclusion are important opportunities to present and then reinforce the workshop theme as well as the goals and objectives. The specific elements to be included in an introduction and overview and in a workshop conclusion are presented in Chapter 6.

The middle of the workshop, in between the introduction and the conclusion, will contain the learning activities that form the heart of the workshop experience. When you design the overall structure, endeavor not only to choose appropriate activities, but to structure them in a way that leads to the conclusion and reinforces your chosen theme. As many business presentation manuals advise, think about "designing the close first" (e.g., D'Arcy, 1992; Morrisey, Sechrest, & Warman, 1997; Peoples, 1992).

➤ *In the workshops you plan to present, how can you use the introduction and conclusion to reinforce the theme and tie the workshop together?*

Including Different Types of Learning Activities

Chapter 2 describes two potential workshop design strategies called "something for everyone" and "measure and match." We have found that for many workshop topics and participant groups, it is appropriate to use the something-for-everyone strategy combined with Kolb's model of individual learning styles. The resulting design strategy described here emphasizes the use of four different types of learning activities corresponding to four learning styles. We refer to these four types of activities as reflecting on experience, assimilating and conceptualizing, experimenting and practicing, and planning for application. These activities correspond to the needs of Imaginative, Analytic, Common Sense, and Dynamic Learners. Figure 4.1 illustrates the relationship between individual learning styles and teaching-learning activities.

Inclusion of all four types of activities contributes to the creation of a complete learning experience in two ways. First, the primary learning needs of all of your participants are met. Second, participants are encouraged to learn in different ways that complement and reinforce their preferred learning styles. If this design strategy is combined with the use of a consistent theme, the same theme can be learned and reinforced in four different and complementary learning experiences. Figure 4.2 summarizes the most important features of each of these four types of learning activities. General descriptions of these activities are provided next. Guidelines for designing specific activities and examples of activities of each type are provided in Chapter 5.

Reflecting-on-Experience Activities

Reflecting-on-experience activities are used to capture the motivation, imagination, and energy of a workshop audience. Such activities create the opportunity to reflect on past experience and apply it to the current learning

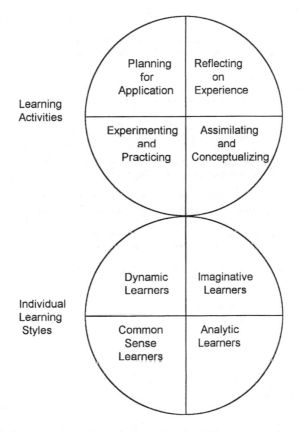

Figure 4.1. Correspondence Between Learning Activities and Individual Learning Styles

situation. Reflecting activities encourage participants to reflect on their own professional and personal behavior in a way that prepares them for new learning and change. These activities begin by affirming what participants already know (McCarthy, 1990). Reflecting learning activities illustrate how participants can benefit from a workshop and how the workshop can be enhanced by active participation. Reflecting often is used at the beginning of a workshop or at a transition from one topic to another.

Reflecting learning activities best correspond to the needs of Imaginative Learners and are essential to these learners. Imaginative Learners learn best when they can attach personal meaning to a learning experience, so

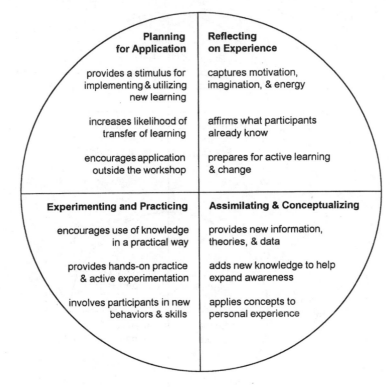

Figure 4.2. Characteristics of Learning Activities

reflecting can help catch their attention and motivate them for learning. However, reflecting activities are also important for capturing the motivation of all workshop participants, particularly at transition points.

➤ *What kinds of learning activities are you familiar with that encourage participants to reflect on their own experience?*

Assimilating and Conceptualizing Activities

Assimilating and conceptualizing activities are used to provide workshop participants with new information. These activities add knowledge to help participants expand their awareness. Assimilating learning activities can provide outside information in the form of theories, data, and facts or can inform the group about itself or individuals about themselves. Assimilating activities also encourage participants to examine current theories and practice critically. For example, a workshop facilitator can report research results related to the topic, survey the audience, and discuss the group's attitudes toward the topic, or have participants complete an instrument or questionnaire that informs individuals about their own attitudes.

In addition to the introduction of new factual information, this quadrant includes the application of concepts to one's own experience. This process of conceptualization is a particularly important aspect of experiential learning that can be emphasized in workshops. If didactic information is presented in an isolated manner, an important opportunity is missed. It is vital to provide opportunities to relate the material that is being taught as directly as possible to the lives of the participants. Relating this material to the participants' own experiences increases motivation and begins to bridge the gap from abstract conceptualization to active experimentation. Assimilating learning activities correspond most closely to the needs of Analytic Learners because these activities provide desired facts as well as offering opportunities for reflection and theory building. However, assimilating activities also are important because they provide a knowledge base for all participants.

➤ *Can you recall activities that do a good job of both presenting didactic content and encouraging learners to use this content to conceptualize their own experience?*

Experimenting and Practicing Activities

 Experimenting and practicing activities encourage participants to use new knowledge in a practical way. These activities provide an opportunity for participants to practice and involve themselves in new behaviors, skills, and knowledge. Therefore, the workshop can provide a safe environment for participants to try out new things before applying them outside in the "real world." Experimenting activities are often paired with assimilating activities so that new knowledge can be put to immediate practical use. For instance, a set of strategies or skills introduced in an assimilating activity can be practiced using role-playing as a part of an experimenting activity. Experimenting learning activities best meet the primary needs of Common Sense Learners by allowing for hands-on practice and active experimentation. Experimenting activities also provide a context for all workshop participants to make the transition from abstract to active learning.

➤ *What kinds of activities are you familiar with that allow learners to experiment with new ideas and practice new skills?*

Planning-for-Application Activities

Planning-for-application activities provide a stimulus for implementing and utilizing new learning outside the workshop context. Planning activities prepare participants for and increase the likelihood of transfer of learning. Because application will, by definition, occur after the workshop ends, planning activities can be seen as preparation and encouragement for application rather than application itself. It is important to attend to the process of application so that workshop learning is not lost when participants leave. These activities often are used at the conclusion of a workshop or when the focus of the workshop is about to shift from one topic to another. Planning activities correspond most directly to the needs of Dynamic Learners, who learn best when provided opportunities to take knowledge out of traditional learning settings and work at applying it to their own lives. Planning activities also allow all participants to take the workshop "home" with them.

➤ *Can you identify activities that do a good job of preparing participants to apply new learning in their own lives after a workshop?*

➤ *When you think of the workshops you have attended or presented, which types of activities have typically been emphasized? Which types of activities have been neglected?*

Sequencing Learning Activities

Kolb's Cycle of Learning

Learning activities should be sequenced so they fit together in a meaningful and memorable way. If you are using learning activities from all four quadrants, it may be best to sequence activities in the same order that they have just been presented. Kolb (1984) suggested that "the process of experiential learning can be described as a four-stage cycle involving four adaptive learning modes—concrete experience, reflective observation, abstract conceptualization, and active experimentation" (p. 40). Kolb's cycle of learning represents a logical approach to sequencing workshop activities because it starts with past experience and ends by looking toward the future. Beginning a workshop by reflecting on experience encourages participants to tap into what they already know, formally or informally, about the topic. With that foundation established, it often is useful to add assimilating and conceptualizing activities in which new information is introduced and synthesized with existing knowledge from experience. Once this new information has been introduced, you may want to proceed to experimenting and practicing so that the new knowledge or skills can be practiced and reinforced in a "laboratory" setting. Concluding a workshop with activities that encourage planning for application emphasizes the importance of transferring workshop learning into participants' personal or professional lives.

Having workshop participants move through Kolb's cycle of learning one time represents the most basic approach to structuring a workshop. This cycle would, of course, be preceded by an introduction and overview and followed by a conclusion. This basic workshop structure is depicted in Exhibit 4.1.

➤ *Would this structure be helpful in organizing the workshops that you are likely to design in the future? Why or why not?*

Alternate Workshop Sequences

There may be some workshops for which a different sequence or structure would be preferable. Your decisions about design alterations will be based on experience and personal preferences. We would like to share one alternative to a standard cycle of learning to prompt your thinking about experimenting with different sequences. We have found two situations in which it makes sense to present an assimilating activity before a reflecting activity at the beginning of a workshop. First, for some topics, all of the participants may not have personal experience on which to reflect. In this situation, an assimilating activity can be used to create a common experience on which the group can then reflect. For example, in a sexual harassment workshop, it is hoped that not all of the participants have personally experienced sexual harassment. It may be best to present a modeling role-play, case study, or read-around (see Chapter 5) of a sexual harassment scenario and then have group members record or share their reactions. When participants are asked to reflect together on the same

EXHIBIT 4.1

Basic Workshop Structure Based on Kolb's Cycle of Learning

1. Introduction and Overview
2. Reflecting on Experience
3. Assimilating and Conceptualizing
4. Experimenting and Practicing
5. Planning for Application
6. Conclusion

stimulus, they are more likely to have complementary perceptions than when each person is reflecting on a different experience.

The second situation that may call for placing assimilation before reflection is when workshop participants are being introduced to a new area in which they may have insufficient background knowledge. In this case, the experience on which you want participants to reflect may be dependent upon technical jargon or unfamiliar concepts. In order for the reflection activity to be successful, you may need to present definitions or other background information in an assimilating activity before encouraging reflection. For example, in an assertiveness workshop, you might provide definitions for passive, assertive, and aggressive behavior and then facilitate a reflecting activity in which participants identify circumstances where they are likely to use each type of behavior.

Obviously, there are numerous other ways to vary your workshop structure, and we encourage you to experiment with different sequences as you gain experience as a designer. If you are an experienced workshop facilitator, you may already recognize situations in which you would want to deviate from the experiential learning cycle. If you are a beginning facilitator, we suggest that you start with the basic workshop structure and later experiment with other sequences when they seem appropriate.

➤ *Based on the topics that you are likely to present, can you think of ways you might want your workshop structure to deviate from the standard cycle of learning?*

Other Strategies for Sequencing Activities

In contrast to sequencing activities according to the type of learning that is encouraged, there also are alternative methods of organization. D'Arcy

(1992) suggests several possible organizational patterns for workshop design, such as sequencing activities by chronology, topic, pros and cons, causes and effects, or problems and solutions. A workshop on management strategies organized chronologically might review different trends in management across the decades and emphasize the lessons learned from each trend. A violence prevention workshop organized around problems and solutions might present several different theories about the causes of violence and then encourage participants to explore possible solutions that might be responsive to the proposed causes. There are workshops where the topic itself might suggest an organization or sequence. For example, a workshop for graduate students on writing a master's thesis might be organized around tips for writing the introduction, literature review, methodology, results, and discussion.

➤ *What kind of structure or sequence has been used in the workshops you have presented or attended? What type of structure or sequence do you hope to use in future workshops?*

Designing Workshops of Different Lengths

During a short workshop of 1 to 2 hours' duration it may be sufficient to complete one full cycle of learning by providing activities in each of the four quadrants. During a half-day or longer workshop, you will probably have time to do more than a standard, one-cycle design. We will share three different strategies for expansion of your workshop design beyond a single cycle of learning. First, you can add one or more additional activities corresponding to one or more learning quadrants. For example, during a half-day workshop, after an initial reflecting activity, you may be able to provide two assimilating activities, each followed by an experimenting activity, before concluding with a planning activity. If you choose this structure and provide two different conceptual models during assimilating, you may want to provide different types of experimenting activities that respond to distinct learning preferences (see Chapter 2). For example, if your first experimenting activity is particularly extroverted, you should probably provide a more introverted activity for the second experimentation.

A second way to expand beyond a single learning cycle is to repeat all four quadrants, creating two or more complete cycles. For example, in a full-day workshop you may want to break the topic into two parts with distinct themes and objectives and complete one four-quadrant learning cycle in the morning followed by a second cycle in the afternoon. In this case, it also is helpful at the end of the afternoon to integrate the two distinct themes.

A third way to design longer workshops is to use Kolb's (1984) cycle of learning for part of your workshop and to use a different design strategy for another part. The alternate design strategy you choose might be one of those described by D'Arcy (1992) based on chronology, topic, pros and cons, causes and effects, or problems and solutions.

You also could organize part of a longer workshop based on the measure-and-match strategy or a something-for-everyone strategy based on another learning model (see Chapter 2). For example, a day-long workshop on personality type could use a standard cycle-of-learning structure in the morning to present and teach about participants' results on the Myers-Briggs Type Indicator. In the afternoon, the group could be divided into smaller groups based on personality type to participate in activities specially designed for each group's personality. This afternoon segment would represent a measure-and-match design that would complement and expand on the morning's something-for-everyone structure (see Chapter 2).

➤ *What length workshops do you anticipate presenting? How will this impact your design strategy?*

Sample Workshop Outline

To conclude this chapter on creating comprehensive workshop designs, we'd like to share a sample outline with you to begin to flesh out some details. This outline is displayed in Exhibit 4.2 and represents a brief (2- to 4-hour) workshop on the topic of diversity and follows a standard one-cycle design strategy.

Summary

The overall structure of a workshop was discussed in this chapter. Important considerations include choosing a consistent theme based on goals and objectives; planning the beginning, middle, and end of the workshop; providing different types of learning activities; and choosing an appropriate

EXHIBIT 4.2
Sample Workshop Outline for a Brief Diversity Workshop

A. **Introduction and Overview**
   1. Introduce yourself and your interest and experience related to the topic.
   2. Preview the workshop theme, goals, and objectives.
   3. Invite all participants to introduce themselves and share what they would like to gain from the workshop.

B. **Reflecting on Experience**
   1. Ask participants to recall a time when they had a misunderstanding based on culture or gender and have them write down answers to a few stimulus questions.
   2. Encourage participants to share in pairs about their experiences.
   3. Invite participants to generate, in a large group, a list of common themes that emerged from this reflection and sharing.

C. **Assimilating and Conceptualizing**
   1. Present a theory or model of diversity. Provide a handout. Lead a discussion.
   2. Ask participants to fill out a brief survey that helps them conceptualize their own experience according to this model.

D. **Experimenting and Practicing**
   1. Hand out sample scenarios in which conflicts arise because of culture or gender.
   2. Encourage small groups to brainstorm possible responses to the situations.
   3. Invite one of the small groups to role-play their solution and solicit feedback from the other participants.

E. **Planning for Application**
   1. Ask the large group to brainstorm ways that the workshop content can be used to decrease cultural conflicts.
   2. Encourage new behavior outside of the workshop by having participants complete action plan worksheets in which they identify ways they would like to change their own behavior.
   3. Invite participants to pair off and share one item on their action plan with one another.

F. **Conclusion**
   1. Thank the group members for their participation.
   2. Answer any final questions. Ask for verbal feedback.
   3. Distribute and collect evaluations.

sequence for the activities. The chapter concluded by considering workshops of different lengths and presenting a sample workshop outline.

Planning for Application

Think about the next workshop you will present. Go through the steps described in this chapter and answer the following questions:

1. What will be the theme or themes of your workshop?

_____

2. How will you begin and end your workshop?

_____

3. What types of workshop activities would you like to include?

_____

4. In what sequence will you present these activities?

_____

Chapter

5

Designing Effective Workshop Learning Activities

At the beginning of the last chapter, workshop design was conceptually divided into two sequential tasks—creating an overall structure for the workshop and designing specific learning activities. These two processes were compared to building a house and then filling it with useful furnishings. The design of particular activities that will meet the goals and objectives of the workshop is the topic of this chapter. If the design of the overall structure of the workshop is like the work of an architect, then the task described here is like the work of an interior designer. Now that the general structure has been set, what will the individual "rooms" in our workshop look like? What will be the style and color of the activities that we provide for our workshop participants? How can we create an inviting environment in which our workshop participants can learn?

To answer these questions, this chapter discusses the process of designing four different types of teaching-learning activities for use in workshops. You might think of these as different types of rooms. It may take different strategies to decorate a living room than a bedroom or a kitchen. Guidelines for designing four types of activities will be presented, and you will be encouraged to practice designing activities for the workshop topics that you are likely to present in the future. After guiding you through this method of creating your own learning activities, a "catalog" of specific descriptions and examples is provided. As you approach the task of designing your own workshops, you will have the opportunity to start from scratch or to adapt "tried and true" activities to your particular topic and group.

Reflecting on Workshop Activities

1. Can you identify a workshop activity or exercise that stands out for you as particularly effective?

_____

2. Why does this particular activity stand out? What made it meaningful for you?

_____

What Are Learning Activities?

A crucial part of designing effective workshops is choosing what the participants will do. Our model of workshop design proposes that, by applying knowledge of experiential learning and learning styles, you can design activities that match the learning preferences of your participants and create a holistic learning experience. Designing effective learning activities allows workshops to be custom tailored to particular topics and groups of participants.

We refer to workshop exercises as learning activities, but they might more accurately be called "teaching-learning activities." This reflects the idea that processes of teaching and learning occur in workshops simultaneously. It may be helpful to think about the traditional distinction between teaching and learning as occurring on a teeter-totter—sometimes you, the facilitator, are more active and the balance will tip toward teaching; at other times, the participants are more active and the balance tips toward learning. Ideally, teaching and learning will be happening continuously throughout a workshop. For the sake of utility, we will use the shorter label, "learning activities," throughout the rest of the book although the teaching process within these activities remains implied.

Descriptions of four types of learning activities were provided in Chapter 4. Now it is time to learn how to design your own activities in each of these quadrants. You will be asked to answer questions that encourage you to think about these four types of activities before you go through a step-by-step process for designing your own.

Beginning to Design Learning Activities

We encourage you to think about how to design specific workshop activities. Please reflect on your experience as a workshop facilitator or participant as you answer the following questions:

1. What can a facilitator do to encourage participants to reflect on relevant past experience (reflecting activities)?

2. What can a facilitator do to promote the learning of new didactic information (assimilating activities)?

3. What can a facilitator do to create opportunities for practicing and actively working with new knowledge (experimenting activities)?

4. What can a facilitator do to encourage participants to apply their new knowledge to their lives after they leave the workshop (planning activities)?

It may have been difficult to answer some of these questions, because the choice of activities depends on the workshop you are presenting. However, we want you to have some practice with the general idea of the four types of activities before we ask you to consider specific topics. Now try designing activities for the following workshop situations:

1. You are beginning a workshop on cultural diversity and you want to encourage participants to think about their personal experiences before addressing more information-oriented learning. What are your ideas for a reflecting activity?

2. You have been asked to present a workshop on personal safety and are interested in providing information about the incidence of crime in your city, yet want to do more than just read off a list of statistics. Please list some ideas for an assimilating activity.

_____

3. Toward the end of a workshop on computer skills, you are interested in allowing participants an opportunity to try out some of the programs you have demonstrated. What can you do for this experimenting activity?

_____

4. In a workshop focused on retirement planning, you want to encourage participants to utilize their new learning after the workshop. Please identify some possibilities for a planning activity.

_____

Now that you've gotten a taste of identifying different types of activities, we will look at designing specific learning activities in a more formal way. In the sections that follow, we will highlight each type of activity, provide you some guidelines for design and the opportunity to practice, and then offer ideas for future application.

Designing Reflecting-on-Experience Activities

To design a reflecting activity, you need some information about the workshop itself. Consider the following initial questions:

1. What is the topic?
2. What are the goals, learning objectives, and/or theme?
3. What kind of interaction do you want to promote?
4. What kind of experience have participants probably had with the topic?

As you review this information about your upcoming workshop, use it to help answer the next set of questions:

5. At what point in the workshop will this activity occur?

6. What types of past experiences do you want to access?
7. What are some commonalities in participants' experiences?
8. What is the best way to access this experience?
9. What kind of format will best fit the overall workshop?
   a. Active or passive?
   b. Directly related to the topic or not?
   c. Interactive or not?
   d. Simple or complex?

For example, if you have been asked to do a 2-hour workshop on communication skills, you might conclude the following:

1. The topic is interpersonal communication skills.
2. The goal and learning objectives include providing information and practice related to communication skills, with a special emphasis on communication in the workplace.
3. Because the workshop participants are an intact work group, you want to promote different types of communication among participants within the context of the workshop as well as afterwards.
4. It is likely that participants have had a great deal of experience with positive and negative workplace communication with each other as well as with other people.

As you look over these initial bits of information, you also may conclude the following:

5. You want this particular reflecting activity to occur at the beginning of the workshop.
6. You want participants to think about their own past communication behavior, particularly at work.
7. You hope to address the theme, "We all have strengths and weaknesses in communication."
8. You want participants to identify their strengths and weaknesses and begin to bring these ideas into the workshop.
9. You want this activity to be semiprivate, to facilitate honesty, but also to involve some level of interaction. You want this to be a fairly simple exercise that, hopefully, not only will get the participants interested in the topic but also primed for the information and practice you will incorporate later in the workshop.

So, as you take in all of this information, you might decide to use the following activity to begin your workshop: Provide worksheets to all of the

EXHIBIT 5.1

Reflecting Activity Design

1. Topic?
2. Goals/learning objectives?
3. Interaction pattern?
4. Relevant participant experiences?
5. When will this activity occur?
6. Types of experiences to access?
7. Themes?
8. How to access the experience?
9. Format issues:
   a. Active/passive?
   b. On topic/not?
   c. Interactive/not?
   d. Simple/complex?
10. Other important issues or concerns?

Some reflecting activities I could use include the following:

---

participants, with the following four sentence stems: "A time when I communicated really well with my coworkers was . . .," "A time when I communicated poorly with my coworkers was . . .," "Things that help me communicate well at work include . . .," and "The following things get in the way of communicating well at work . . ." Give plenty of room between the sentence stems for answers to be written. Participants can write down the answers privately, but then will be asked to share their answers with a partner in the second half of the activity.

Now, we'd like to give you the opportunity to try to design a reflecting activity for a workshop that you will do. Have a specific workshop in mind as you answer the questions in Exhibit 5.1.

If you have trouble identifying activities on your own in this section, don't worry. Later on in this chapter we will provide you with lists and examples of each type of teaching-learning activity.

Have you completed the worksheet? Congratulations! You've designed a reflecting activity for your workshop. For a little more practice, we encourage you to identify another topic for which you may need to design reflecting activities and begin to think through the questions we have provided.

What are some additional topics for which you'd like practice designing reflecting activities? Please take a moment to write down your answer to the questions and your ideas for activities.

Designing Assimilating and Conceptualizing Activities

Think of times when you have facilitated or participated in an activity that provided participants with new information. What did you or the facilitator do in these instances?

The types of questions you ask yourself in order to design an assimilating activity include many of those identified in the previous section on designing reflecting activities. For instance, you will, of course, always need to be aware of the topic of the presentation, when you want the activity to occur, and so on. Some particular questions relevant to assimilating activities include the following:

1. What is the information you want to share with the participants?
2. Do you want to provide outside theories, data, facts, or inside information about the group itself?
3. Do you want to facilitate information about individual participants or the group as a whole?
4. Do you want to be the main presenter of the information or should the process be more interactive and interpersonal, with participants providing information as well?
5. Will you utilize questionnaires or other instruments?
6. Do you want to utilize movement around the room as a learning tool?
7. Are there different ways to present the information, such as via videos, overheads, handouts, and so on?

Now, choose a topic for which you will design an assimilating activity. Use a separate piece of paper to answer the questions listed above, as well as to list any additional relevant information. (We will not provide worksheets for the remaining activities as we did for the reflecting activities, although we encourage you to develop your own if you found the worksheet a helpful tool.)

After reviewing the above information, decide on one or two assimilating activities you could use and write down these ideas. Again, we encourage you to identify additional topics and practice designing more assimilating and conceptualizing activities on your own paper.

Designing Experimenting and Practicing Activities

Experimenting and practicing is an area that is frequently left out of workshops, so it may be tougher to identify the experimenting activities in which you have participated. Think of times when you have been in a setting that has allowed you to work with new knowledge in a practical, hands-on way. Or, think of a time when you, as a workshop facilitator, allowed participants to try out new skills. What took place that encouraged this kind of personal interaction with the knowledge?

_____

In addition to the basic questions about topic and goals, and so on, some specific questions that will help you design experimenting activities are as follows:

1. How realistic do you want the practice situation to be? How can you "set the stage"?
2. Do you want to provide the context or have participants create it?
3. Do you want to direct the process of practice or have participants govern it?
4. Do you want to use scripts, handouts, worksheets?
5. Do you want to use drawing, painting, working with clay, and so forth, to facilitate the exercise?
6. Do you want to utilize movement in the activity?
7. Will this be an individual, small-group, or large-group exercise?

Now, choose a topic for which you will design an experimenting activity. Using your own paper, answer the questions listed above and list any additional relevant information.

After reviewing this information, decide on some possible experimenting activities and write down your ideas.

Now identify additional topics to design more experimenting and practicing activities, answer the questions listed above, and identify possible activities.

Designing Planning-for-Application Activities

Think of a time when a workshop facilitator helped you apply new knowledge to your "real life." What did that facilitator do to help you take knowledge home?

As mentioned previously, the majority of planning activities help participants think about how they will utilize the new information after they leave the workshop. The following questions will help you design planning activities:

1. Is it appropriate to give participants specific assignments to ensure that they apply the knowledge?
2. Do you want to have the group identify ways that they can utilize the knowledge or have participants work on this individually?
3. Do you want participants to set specific goals for application?
4. Do you want participants to commit to action privately or out loud? On paper or just mentally?
5. If this is the rare occasion where the workshop is a real-life setting (e.g., a business communication workshop with an intact work group), how do you want to utilize this situation? For instance, participants could make specific agreements with each other for future behavior.

Now, choose a topic or existing workshop for which you need a planning activity. Use a separate piece of paper to answer the questions listed above, as well as to list any additional relevant information. After reviewing the information, decide on what you will do for your planning activity or activities for your workshop. Write down your ideas.

What are some additional topics or existing workshops for which you want to design some planning for application activities? Write down your ideas for these activities.

Specific Examples of Learning Activities

Now that you have learned to design your own learning activities, we will share some of our favorites. Some of the following activities are ones we have designed ourselves, but many are exercises we learned about elsewhere. It is important to note that entire books have been written on some of the following activities and techniques and that our descriptions are certainly not intended to replicate these more comprehensive resources. Rather, we've briefly described and explained each activity and provided selected references when appropriate for those readers who desire further elaboration.

Examples of Reflecting Activities

Icebreakers

Icebreakers (e.g., Berry & Kaufman, 1994; Dahmer, 1992; Pfeiffer, 1990, p. 10) are brief interactive exercises that encourage and prepare participants for interpersonal learning during a workshop. Icebreakers may be unrelated to the topic and simply used to "break the ice." If an icebreaker is directly related to the workshop topic, it has the added benefit of being a "motivation grabber." These activities are usually more appealing to extroverts than introverts.

Example: Tape the names of famous people to participants' backs so that others can read each participant's identity but he or she cannot. Participants are asked to mingle with others and ask yes-or-no questions until they discover their own identities.

Example: At the beginning of a leadership workshop, read famous quotes about leadership and ask participants to guess who they think was the original source of the quote. Whoever gets the most right wins a small prize.

Dyadic or Small-Group Sharing

Dyadic or small-group sharing is a simple but effective way to encourage reflection by asking participants to pair off and share with one another about their past experiences related to the workshop topic. Dyadic sharing can be simply verbal or can be preceded by written reflection. The facilitator can provide specific sentence stems or broader topics for sharing.

Example: During a workshop on self-esteem, have participants share in dyads the answers to several sentence stems like, "I feel best about myself when . . ." and "One thing that leads to problems with my self-esteem is . . ."

Example: In a teaching-skills workshop, ask participants to write down three sayings or slogans that best describe their philosophy of teaching. Then have participants share these slogans in small groups and discuss them in terms of the teaching skills they want to refine in the workshop.

Stimulus Role-Plays

Stimulus role-plays (Obear, 1991) are preplanned role-plays structured by the facilitators and presented to the participants. Stimulus role-plays are designed to stimulate thinking and provide a relevant example upon which to reflect.

Example: At the beginning of a workshop on communication styles, the two facilitators feign misunderstanding each other as they begin to present. The confusion escalates for a while, and then the facilitators let participants in on the ruse. Discussion then focuses on what it was like for participants to witness the misunderstanding and asks what could have been done to circumvent the problem.

Example: At the beginning of a workshop about sexual orientation, facilitators role-play a discussion between a gay or lesbian person and a coworker who asks questions about his or her personal life assuming he or she is heterosexual.

Gallery Exercises

Gallery exercises are used to prompt reflection on a workshop topic. Pictures related to the workshop theme are displayed and participants are asked to respond to the images. Slide show presentations can serve a similar purpose, although slides allow for less direct interaction among participants and between participants and the images. Gallery exercises are responsive to the needs of visual learners.

Example: In an introductory workshop for graduate teaching assistants, display images of recent campus events alongside excerpts from teaching evaluations, reports of student ACT/SAT scores, and student demographic summaries. After all participants have looked at the entire gallery, elicit verbal responses and facilitate a discussion on the nature of "today's student."

Example: In an alcohol awareness workshop, display images of alcohol from the media to highlight societal messages about alcohol use. Ask participants to write their responses on Post-it notes and stick them next to the images. After participants have responded, ask them to circle the gallery again and read others' responses.

Brainstorming

Brainstorming (e.g., Szczypkowski, 1980, p. 58) is a method of generating a variety of ideas related to a workshop topic. Responses are generated without evaluation in order to encourage original and creative ideas.

Example: In a workshop designed to teach fund-raising skills, ask participants to brainstorm all of the potential sources of contributions they can think of.

Example: In a time management workshop, ask participants to brainstorm a list of reasons why people procrastinate.

Guided Fantasies

Guided fantasies (e.g., Bourne, 1990) are used to assist participants in imagining scenarios related to the workshop topic. Participants are asked to relax and close their eyes, and the facilitator verbally encourages them to imagine different scenes and experiences. Guided fantasies may be particularly helpful for intuitive and feeling learners.

Example: In a career decision-making workshop, ask participants to imagine a day in the future. Guide participants through different parts of the day related to work and personal life. In processing the fantasy, ask participants to reflect on what they imagined and how it might impact their current decision making.

Example: In a stress management workshop, guide participants through specific stressful situations. Instruct them to envision themselves handling the stress in an appropriate and healthy manner, which you describe.

Games

Games (e.g., Pfeiffer, 1990, p. 10) are engaging activities used to activate participants' thoughts about the topic. Games tend to be enjoyed by extroverted participants.

Example: As the initial activity in a career-change workshop, have participants toss a ball among themselves. As each participant catches the ball, she or he is required to call out his or her "secret" dream job.

Example: In a team-building workshop for university residence life professionals, give participants Bingo-style game cards with items like "My first professional job was in residence life," "I never worked in the cafeteria," and "Sometimes I like doing rounds." Within a short time period, participants must find individuals for whom the statement is true and get their signatures on the handout.

Storytelling

Storytelling is a way to provide a common experience on which the group can reflect together and that can provide insights related to the workshop topic. After telling a story, the facilitator can lead a discussion or point out the lessons to be learned from the story. Story content can be metaphorical or overtly related to the topic. Facilitators can use traditional fables or fairy tales or make up their own stories. Storytelling represents an activity that encourages auditory learning.

Example: In a workshop on motivation, tell a story about someone who overcame adversity in several ways and then ask participants to identify the motivating strategies used.

Example: In a workshop on men's issues, read the ancient story "Iron John" and then use it to highlight different aspects of men's mental, emotional, and spiritual development.

Music

Music can be used to encourage participants to relate to a topic on a more emotional level than might be accessed with information alone. Songs with lyrics related to the topic are helpful in setting a mood. Auditory learners are particularly responsive to music.

Example: While doing artwork in a workshop focusing on father-son relationships, play songs with relevant themes in the background. For example, "Cat's in the Cradle" by Harry Chapin (1985) or "Father and Son" by Cat Stevens (1970).

Example: As new residence advisors enter a confrontation skills workshop, play music with themes of defying authority to introduce some humor into the topic. For example, "The Authority Song" by John Cougar (1983) or "I Can't Drive 55" by Sammy Hagar (1984).

Examples of Assimilating Activities

Lectures/Lecturettes

Lectures (e.g., Cooper & Heenan, 1980, p. 41) are used to provide factual content information about the workshop topic. A short lecture is called a "lecturette" (Pfeiffer, 1990). Lectures and lecturettes represent a form of auditory learning.

Example: In a workshop on educational assessment, present new assessment techniques to participants via lecture format.

Example: In a stress management workshop, provide factual information about the physiological effects of anxiety.

Group Surveys

Group surveys (e.g., Angelo & Cross, 1993, pp. 255-316) are a way to provide participants with topic-relevant information about the group itself.

Example: At an employee training session focused on budgeting skills, administer a survey to assess knowledge of various budget-related issues. Share the results with the participants and also use them to guide the focus of the remainder of the training session.

Example: In a sexual assault prevention workshop, survey participants' attitudes using a brief questionnaire and then tally the results. Give feedback to the audience highlighting gender differences in attitudes about sexual assault.

Values Clarification

Values clarification (e.g., Brock, 1991; Gay, 1994; Proudman, 1992) exercises allow participants to explore their own values and experiences and how they differ from those of other participants in an involving and nonthreatening way.

Example: In a multicultural workshop, read a series of diversity-related statements and ask participants to move to one of the four corners of the room labeled: "Yes," "No," "Maybe," and "No Comment." An example of a diversity values statement might be: "I am equally comfortable spending time with people of my own race and people of other races." This values clarification activity is called "Four Corners."

Example: In a session focused on management techniques, provide information on several types of management styles, then encourage participants to discuss their personal reactions to each style from both management and labor perspectives.

Questionnaires/Instruments

Questionnaires or instruments (e.g., Pfeiffer, 1990, p. 11) allow participants to gain new knowledge about themselves. Questionnaires are a way to access information about participants that does not require verbal participation.

Example: In a staff development workshop, use the Myers-Briggs Type Indicator (Briggs & Myers, 1988) to explore individual personality type and how it impacts the work setting and group dynamics.

Example: In a workshop focusing on facilitation skills, ask participants to fill out a brief instrument designed to assess their use of various facilitation skills.

Modeling Role-Plays

Modeling role-plays (e.g., Knox, 1986, p. 89) are used to demonstrate effective behavior related to the workshop topic. They can be presented by the facilitators or by volunteer participants.

Example: In an assertiveness workshop, facilitators perform a role-play demonstrating personal limit setting.

Example: In a social skills workshop, facilitators perform a role-play demonstrating initiating and continuing a conversation with a stranger.

Case Studies

Case studies (e.g., Boyce, 1995; Pfeiffer, 1990, p. 9) are accounts of actual events related to workshop topics that are used to prompt exploration and discussion. Case studies may appeal to needs of sensing learners.

Example: In a fraternity leadership workshop, use reports of incidents involving hazing and alcohol use to promote discussion.

Example: In a workshop focused on body image, present examples of celebrities who have struggled with eating disorders to illustrate the universality of body image problems.

Movement/Sorting

Movement or sorting exercises have people move to different areas of a room, or to stand or sit, to indicate different experiences or opinions and to highlight the diversity within the group. Movement and sorting exercises are often a good way to promote values clarification. These exercises encourage kinesthetic learning.

Example: In a program highlighting the impact of alcohol use on relationships, ask participants to form a human continuum from one end of the room to the other, with the two end-points labeled "completely agree" and "completely disagree." Read statements such as, "A woman who gets drunk is asking to be raped," and ask participants to respond to each statement by physically placing themselves at the place on the continuum that corresponds to their opinion.

Example: In a diversity workshop, ask members of different cultural groups (ethnic minorities, sexual minorities, differing socioeconomic backgrounds) sequentially by group to stand when an aspect of their background is identified by the facilitator. Use this to illustrate the common occurrence of multiple identities.

Fishbowl Discussions

Fishbowl discussions (e.g., Loughary & Hopson, 1979, p. 92; Priles, 1993) are structured exercises in which a group of participants sits in a circle while another group silently observes from outside the circle. These activities are used to help participants gain knowledge about the group itself. Fishbowl discussions allow participants in the observer role to gain "inside information" from another group that might not be expressed in an open, between-groups discussion. An open discussion can follow the fishbowl focusing on why different groups have different perceptions or experiences.

Example: In a workshop on sexual harassment, ask the female participants to discuss their fears about being sexually harassed while male participants listen silently. Subsequently, male participants sit inside the circle and discuss their feelings about being perceived as potential harassers while the female participants listen.

Example: In a diversity workshop, ask members of minority groups to discuss their experiences with discrimination in the organization in the circle while majority individuals listen. Next, ask the majority individuals to sit inside the circle and discuss their experiences with discrimination.

Read-Arounds

Read-arounds ask participants to read aloud excerpts, scenarios, or other information related to the workshop topic. Read-arounds facilitate auditory learning.

Example: In a workshop focusing on customer service, ask each participant to read part of the organization's customer service guidelines or to read suggestions from customers.

Example: In a workshop on racism, ask participants to read a list of white privileges.

Handouts/Overheads

Handouts or overheads are written summaries or graphic depictions of material related to the workshop topic. Handouts are printed on paper and distributed to participants. Overheads are projected on a screen. It is often useful to provide similar information as both overheads and handouts because some participants will prefer to follow your description of the overhead and others will prefer to look at their handouts and make notes on them. Handouts and overheads are used to meet the needs of visual learners.

Example: Present a summary of topic-relevant facts and statistics about the job market during a career development workshop.

Example: Show or distribute examples of different types of résumés during a job search skills workshop.

Videos

Videos (e.g., Knox, 1986, pp. 118-120) are used to present information in an interesting way and/or to include more credible, famous, or entertaining resources.

Example: In an interview skills workshop, present examples of effective and ineffective interview behaviors in a video format.

Example: Present a videotape exploring the negative effects of sexual harassment; the hosts of the program are famous television actors.

Examples of Experimenting Activities

Practice Role-Plays

Practice role-plays (e.g., van Ments, 1992) are used to practice new behaviors or skills related to the workshop topic. Role-plays will generally be enjoyed more by extroverts than introverts and represent an opportunity for kinesthetic learning.

Example: In a social skills workshop, encourage participants to practice different ways of meeting new people.

Example: In an anger management workshop, ask participants to act out anger-provoking situations and then utilize their new skills to resolve the situations.

Simulations

Simulations (e.g., Crookall & Arai, 1995; Gaw, 1996) are used to present realistic or metaphorical situations so participants can practice using knowledge related to the workshop topic.

Example: In a leadership workshop, ask participants to play the roles of members of a selection committee and make decisions about fictitious applicants. This simulation allows participants to identify their own values and decision-making strategies.

Example: Require participants in a diversity workshop to communicate with each other and come to conclusions regarding several exercises. Prior to the exercises, however, provide different participants different "rules of interaction" that they must follow. This inevitably leads to some confusion and frustration, which can set the foundation for a discussion of cultural assumptions and norms.

Worksheets

Worksheets require participants to use knowledge in a written format or to practice writing-based skills. Worksheets allow for introverted and tactile learning.

Example: Encourage participants in a crisis management workshop to plan their own organizational response to crises through a step-by-step worksheet.

Example: In a time management workshop, ask participants to complete a weekly schedule to learn how to budget their time.

Card Sorting

Card sorting can be used to help participants experiment with information that needs to be classified into different categories. Participants are given index cards with topic-related concepts or ideas printed on them and asked to sort them according to criteria identified by the facilitator. Card sorting is a good example of tactile learning.

Example: In a workshop on organizational decision making, give participants cards with different types of decisions made within an organization and ask them to sort the cards into groups according to who should make the decisions. Categories might include individual employees, the director alone, small work groups, or the entire staff.

Example: In a workshop on learning styles, list learning characteristics on cards and ask participants to sort them into groups according to the learning style to which they correspond.

Open Discussions

Open discussions allow participants to share their ideas with one another with little interference from the facilitator. Discussions promote auditory and extroverted learning.

Example: In a workshop on corporate downsizing, present the need for budget cuts and ask participants to discuss their ideas.

Example: In an AIDS prevention workshop, ask participants to discuss how their lives have been impacted, directly or indirectly, by the AIDS crisis.

Structured Discussions

Structured discussions (e.g., Loughary & Hopson, 1979, p. 90) require that the facilitator maintain more guidance or control questions, time limits, or other structures. Structured discussions allow an organized way for participants to share their ideas in an interactive manner. This kind of structure is particularly helpful with difficult subjects.

Example: Ask participants in a wellness program a series of questions highlighting their health practices, leading progressively from information to practical application.

Example: In a Total Quality Management workshop, lead participants through a discussion of their own management styles that highlight TQM principles.

Artwork

Artwork (e.g., Cattaneo, 1994) allows workshop participants creatively to access and express their ideas and experiences related to a workshop topic. Artwork represents a form of tactile and visual learning that may also appeal to feeling learners.

Example: In a family dynamics workshop, ask participants to draw a picture of their families. They can represent their families either realistically or symbolically, including relationships and dynamics, with the use of different shapes, symbols, or colors.

Example: In a smoking cessation workshop, ask participants to draw or otherwise represent their lives before and after they quit smoking.

Scenarios

Scenarios (e.g., Crego & Powell, 1996; Golas, 1995) are exemplary situations that provide specific examples with stimulus questions and are used to activate learning in structured discussions.

Example: In a workshop on gender differences, present the "life stories" of a "typical" man and woman, from birth to adulthood. Highlight differences at each developmental and social stage and encourage participants to reflect on the effects of their own experiences as these life stories are told and discussed.

Example: As a part of a sexual assault prevention workshop, present a scenario of two college students on a date. As different stages of the date are described, ask participants stimulus questions related to communication, decision making, and consent.

Maps

Maps (e.g., Abery, 1994; Angelo & Cross, 1993, pp. 197-202) are graphic depictions of aspects of people's lives. Maps will tend to appeal to visual learners.

Example: To highlight the diversity of participants at a national conference, ask workshop participants to form a map of the United States (and/or the world) in the room, with each participant approximating the location of his or her hometown or birthplace.

Example: In a career decision-making workshop, ask participants to depict the different roles in their lives according to Super's (1987) career-life rainbow. This map is used to illustrate the multiple role demands that must be addressed in career and lifestyle planning.

Time Lines

Time lines (e.g., Brammer, 1992; Hoar, 1994) are graphic depictions of significant life events across time. The events recorded on the time line should be related to the workshop topic. Time lines are likely to appeal to sensing and thinking learners.

Example: Ask participants in a couples communication workshop to construct time lines of their relationships, paying particular attention to the connection between communication difficulties and relevant personal events.

Example: In a career decision-making workshop, construct time lines to represent family events, educational events, personal accomplishments and disappointments, and career-oriented thoughts across participants' lives.

Psychodrama

Psychodramatic experiments (Moreno, 1944) use a range of techniques in which participants represent aspects of themselves or of dynamics present in their lives that are relevant to the workshop topic. This encourages emotional release and insight. Psychodrama represents kinesthetic learning that is most likely to meet the needs of extroverted learners.

Example: In a family dynamics workshop, ask one participant to act as "director" and choose people in the group to represent his family and arrange them in a way that represents their relationships with each other. Ask the director to have the group lay the scene first the way his family used to act and then how he would have liked his family to behave. The experience is processed focusing on family dynamics and emotional impact.

Check-In/Check-Out

Check-in and check-out are used at the beginning, throughout, and especially at the end of the workshops to allow participants to verbalize how they are experiencing information and processes that are a part of the workshop.

Example: In a workshop for survivors of sexual assault, ask participants what they learned about the recovery process from a panel of speakers who are also rape survivors.

Example: After a particularly powerful video depicting the "ethnic cleansing" in the Balkans, give participants time to discuss their emotional reactions before moving on to the next topic.

Examples of Planning Activities

Personal Practice of Skills Learned in Role-Plays

Personal practice of skills learned in role-plays (e.g., Steinert, 1993; van Ments, 1992) provides an opportunity for participants to incorporate knowledge from the workshop into their own personal behaviors. Most workshops will not allow for "real" practice to occur that is not role-playing. However, it is possible when an intact group is participating in a workshop together.

Example: In a staff development presentation focusing on assertiveness in the workplace, have coworkers interact with each other, practicing likely situations they will face when they return to work together.

Example: In a couples' communication workshop, encourage spouses to practice problem solving with one another using skills learned in the workshop.

Action Plans

Action plans (e.g., Anderson, 1995; Gmelch & Chan, 1994) offer participants the opportunity to contract with each other and the facilitators to take knowledge gained in the workshop and apply it to their outside lives. Action plans are likely to appeal to the needs of intuitive learners.

Example: In a time management workshop, ask participants to make plans to complete a project such as a research paper that is actually due in one of their classes. Ask them to plan to use selected techniques learned in the workshop and encourage them to set realistic expectations for themselves. Ask them to record this action plan on a calendar provided as a workshop handout.

Example: At the end of a workshop on fitness, encourage participants to develop a wellness plan for themselves, incorporating areas of nutrition, stress management, and exercise.

Goal Setting

Goal setting involves stating specific, measurable goals and dates when those goals are expected to be accomplished. This specificity increases the likelihood that application will occur.

Example: In a workshop focused on the empowerment of employees, encourage each manager to identify one empowerment technique that she or he will utilize during the next week.

Example: In a job search workshop, ask participants to set goals for when they will write their résumés and how many jobs they will apply for in the coming week.

Brainstorming Solutions

Brainstorming solutions (e.g., Alvino, 1993; Burstyn, 1993) can be used as a way for the group to cooperate in identifying possible solutions to an individual or collective difficulty.

Example: In a social skills workshop, ask participants to brainstorm places where they can meet new people and apply the skills they have learned in the workshop.

Example: In a diversity workshop, encourage participants to brainstorm ways to respond to discrimination in the workplace.

Homework

Homework can be used to provide participants the opportunity to apply knowledge they have learned from the workshop after they leave.

Example: At the end of a management skills workshop, ask the president of the company to stand up and communicate her or his expectation that she or he will be seeing the new management skills in action in the coming weeks.

Example: After a relaxation workshop, ask participants to use learned techniques when experiencing anxiety.

Quizzes

Quizzes allow facilitators to measure how much has been learned by participants and help consolidate material into participants' memory.

Example: After a workshop on leadership styles, give participants a quiz on the characteristics of different leadership techniques.

Example: At the conclusion of an assertiveness workshop, ask participants to recall definitions of different styles of communication.

Speak-Outs

Speak-outs (e.g., Janus, 1992) give participants the opportunity to express verbally how they have been impacted by the workshop.

Example: Ask participants in a diversity workshop to talk about what they have learned about oppression from the workshop.

Example: Ask participants in a presentation skills workshop to identify one new facilitation skill they plan to utilize in the future.

Adaptation of Activities

Our categorization of learning activities into different learning quadrants is based on our experiences and is not absolute. The classification is based on the type of learning we think is most often promoted rather than the structure of the activity itself. Therefore, it is possible for many of the previously listed activities to be modified to facilitate different types of learning. Obviously, the activities can be adapted to address a wide variety of workshop topics.

For example, role-plays can be used to promote all four types of learning. Stimulus role-plays are considered reflecting activities. Modeling role-plays tend to promote assimilation. Practice role-plays are a useful way to encourage experimentation. Personal practice of skills can be used as a planning activity. Similarly, a carefully planned activity may meet more than one type of learning need. For instance, a self-survey about workshop facilitation styles can interest the participants in the topic (reflecting), as well as provide information about different types of facilitation styles (assimilating).

Summary

The first half of this chapter focused on how to design learning activities corresponding to the four learning quadrants. The second half of the chapter provided a catalog of specific examples of learning activities that can be adapted to different workshop topics. Readers were encouraged to think about how to custom design their own activities or to adapt the activities from the catalog for their own use.

Planning for Application

1. Look through the catalog of sample activities and for each learning quadrant identify one new activity that you'd like to try.

_____

2. For each of these chosen activities, identify potential workshop topics for which it would be particularly useful and write out a step-by-step procedure for each.

_____

Directing the Workshop and Creating a Learning Environment

Presenting a workshop involves two complementary roles that we call *directing* and *facilitating*. The directing role involves guiding workshop participants through a series of events and activities during the allotted time, and ensuring that the workshop has a beginning, middle, and end that fit together as a coherent experience. The facilitating role involves using skills and behaviors to promote experiential learning. In short, directing focuses more on the nuts and bolts of what to do, whereas facilitating is more concerned with the process of learning. If directing answers the question "what?" then facilitating answers the question "how?" Although these two roles are conceptually distinct, they involve overlapping behaviors and occur simultaneously. As a workshop presenter, you are both director and facilitator at the same time. The directing role is addressed here in Chapter 6 by describing what will happen throughout the workshop and how to organize and pace the events. The facilitating role is explored in Chapter 7 by describing specific things you can say and do to encourage different types of learning. Although this conceptual distinction regarding directing is made here, in other parts of the book we use the term *facilitator* to encompass both roles.

Chapters 4 and 5 discussed workshop structure and activity design as compared to the work of architects and interior designers. In contrast, workshop direction is more like the work of a carpenter. Now that the plans have been made, how do we begin building? How will we begin to structure this workshop experience? First, we discuss how to create a workshop environment that is conducive to experiential learning. The second half of the chapter is presented in a roughly chronological sequence and addresses beginning the workshop, maintaining a coherent message, pacing and timing, and concluding the workshop. For each of these steps, we make suggestions on how you can create an environment where experiential learning can occur.

Reflecting on Workshop Direction

Before considering our ideas about workshop direction, reflect on your own ideas by answering the following questions:

1. What can you do, as a workshop director, to create a positive learning environment?

   _____

2. What do you think are the most important things for a workshop presenter to do at the beginning of a workshop?

   _____

3. What are some good guidelines for making a workshop go smoothly with regard to timing and pacing?

   _____

4. What do you think is the best way for a presenter to conclude a workshop?

   _____

The Workshop Learning Environment

A crucial component of directing workshops is considering the learning environment you want to create. The learning environment may be more about how a workshop feels than what it looks like. Hiemstra (1991) defined a learning environment as "all of the physical surroundings, psychological or emotional conditions, and social or cultural influences affecting the growth and development of an adult engaged in an educational environment" (p. 8). Different writers have focused on different aspects of the environment that promote and encourage learning. Some have stressed the importance of the physical setting. For example, Vosko (1991) described the impact of seating arrangements, sight lines, and equipment on learning. Other writers have emphasized the importance of psychological or interpersonal variables related to learning environments. Drum and Lawler (1988) suggested that workshops should "take place in a setting conducive to safe, honest interpersonal exchanges, to uninhibited self-exploration, and to hopefulness that the desired change can be made" (p. 71). Knox (1986) highlighted the need for a balance between support and challenge and defined a challenging environment as one that "is problem-centered, is neither boring nor threatening, promotes worthwhile educational achievement, and helps participants understand the problem situation, as well as the problem, and strategies for formulating effective solutions" (p. 132). Knowles (1980) suggested that an educative environment should include "respect for personality, participation in decision making, freedom of expression and availability of information; and mutuality of responsibility in defining goals, planning and conducting activities, and evaluating" (p. 67). Several of the most important aspects of creating a positive learning environment within a workshop are listed in Exhibit 6.1 and will be detailed next.

Arranging the Physical Environment

On the day of a workshop, one of the first considerations is arranging the physical environment. The physical environment will influence the atmosphere and interaction patterns that occur within the workshop. For example, physical arrangement communicates information about levels of both authority and formality. At one extreme is a presenter expressing a formal role of superiority by standing behind a raised podium, in front of an audience seated in rows facing the podium. This arrangement communicates authority and expertise and discourages interaction. At the other extreme is a facilitator who communicates a sense of informality and equality with the participants by sitting in a circle on the same level with the participants. This arrangement communicates equality and encourages interaction between the facilitator and participants. Of course, practical

EXHIBIT 6.1

Important Aspects of a Positive Workshop Environment

Physical environment is comfortable
Relationships are encouraged
Communication is multidirectional
Trust and acceptance are built
Encouragement is provided

considerations such as the size of the group also contribute to these
decisions. For example, if there are more than about 20 participants, sitting
in a circle becomes less practical. A compromise between these two
extremes is a semicircular or U shape with the facilitator at the opening.
Vosko (1991) explored the impact of different seating arrangements and
suggested that in many learning environments, this semicircular seating
arrangement encourages greater participation and interaction than an arrangement that focuses on a single person, such as a lecture hall. This
allows eye contact among participants yet also focuses attention on the
facilitator or an up-front display such as a chalk board or overhead projector. A semicircle also creates a stage area for participant-oriented learning
activities that might occur during experimenting and practicing activities.

Other considerations related to physical arrangements include whether
participants should be seated at a table to create a writing surface or be
seated without a table to remove perceptual barriers between participants.
In addition to the presence of a writing surface, a table suggests a more
formal arrangement and allows less opportunity for observation of nonverbal communication. If your workshop design includes breaking into small
groups or moving around, you will need a bigger room with moveable
furniture to accommodate such groups or movement. A list of physical
environment considerations is presented in Exhibit 6.2.

➤ *What makes a physical environment comfortable for you? What can you do to
ensure physical comfort in your workshops?*

Creating Relationships

Because the workshop environment encourages more interpersonal
learning than many traditional educational environments, it is helpful for

EXHIBIT 6.2
Physical Environment Considerations

Group size
Location and size of room
Level of authority
Level of formality
Seating arrangements
Opportunity for eye contact/sight lines
Need for a writing surface?
Need for movable furniture?

presenters to attend to the creation of relationships. Hiemstra and Sisco (1990) pointed out three types of relationships that contribute to a positive learning environment. They suggested that participants should have relationships with (a) other participants, (b) with the presenter, and (c) with the content of the learning experience. In a traditional learning environment, interpersonal relationships are not valued; it is only the relationship with the content that is emphasized. In a workshop environment, you have the opportunity to create a relationship between yourself and the participants by sharing personal examples of the material and learning from the participants. As a workshop director, you can choose learning activities in which participants interact with one another and learn from other participants. Knox (1986) also stressed relationships by suggesting that a facilitator should help participants get acquainted with one another and by encouraging the facilitator to present himself or herself as a person. Presenting yourself personally includes being "informal enough that participants come to know you as a person" (Knox, 1986, p. 133). Talking about your own personal experiences to illustrate workshop content and presenting yourself as a fellow learner rather than just an authority figure or expert can create more positive rapport within the workshop environment. Davis (1974) suggested that a positive relationship between the facilitator and participants begins when the facilitator takes the time to greet participants and make sure everyone is comfortable at the beginning of a workshop.

It is also important to attend to rapport building throughout the workshop. For instance, at appropriate times, you may share personal anecdotes related to the topic and to point out ways that you have learned through experience. Care should be taken, however, that self-disclosure is moderate, related to the topic, and furthers the goal of learning. For example, in a workshop on substance abuse it may be appropriate for a facilitator to disclose about a past problem with alcohol addiction. However, this same disclosure may be of questionable value in a workshop with a different topic, and might distract from the central themes you are presenting.

➤ *When directing a workshop, what can you do to create a relationship between yourself and the participants? What can you do to create relationships among participants within the workshop?*

Multidirectional Communication

In contrast to traditional learning settings, communication in a workshop is not expected to be unidirectional. An effective workshop presenter should be able to listen and understand as well as express ideas. As a workshop director and facilitator, you should make sure that there is time for participants to share their ideas and for you to listen to their questions, opinions, and experiences. It is helpful to build in opportunities for both formal and informal dialogue to occur throughout a workshop. Informal dialogue with participants throughout the workshop is a way for you to keep the workshop vital and engaging as well as a way to gauge the impact of the workshop.

➤ *When directing a workshop, what can you do to ensure that you listen to your participants? What can you do to ensure that workshop participants listen to one another?*

Building Trust and Acceptance

In order for participants to be able to learn about themselves in a personally relevant manner, they must feel safe and must be able to trust both the presenter and the other participants. If participants do not feel safe in your workshop, it is unlikely that they will fully engage in active and interactive learning. Drum and Lawler (1988) described the three realms in which trust must be created as (a) genuine caring and respect on the part of the presenter, (b) presenter expertise in the form of personal skills and knowledge, and (c) trust between participants. Brookfield (1990) described a similar process of building trust and emphasized the need for both facilitator credibility and authenticity. Credibility is similar to expertise but also includes personal presentation and having something to offer participants. Authenticity includes consistency and congruence, ability to admit errors, and acting as a positive role model. It is an important part of the director's role to attend equally to safe interpersonal interactions and other aspects of the workshop environment and content.

➤ *What makes a new learning environment feel safe to you? What makes an environment feel unsafe? What can you do to increase the sense of trust and acceptance in your workshops?*

Providing Encouragement

Workshop learning is not easy for all people, and different participants will learn in different ways and at different rates (see Chapter 2). Therefore, encouragement must be provided so learning occurs at a pace that meets the needs of the maximum number of participants. Drum and Lawler (1988) identified the four methods for providing encouragement listed below. We've added our own examples to flesh out each point:

1. Projecting confidence that change can occur. "I'm glad you asked about that. This is an area where many people struggle, but I'd like to share some proven strategies with you."
2. Sequencing activities so they proceed from easy to more difficult. "Now that we have mastered the basics this morning, we will proceed to the more challenging situations this afternoon."
3. Using the progress of some participants to encourage others. "That sounds like something that Hannah was telling me about during the break. Hannah, I wonder if you would feel comfortable sharing with Brandon what you've learned?"
4. Attending carefully to the attainable aspects of each participant's goals. "Of the things you've said you want to work on, I think the best place to start to maximize your chances for success is . . ."

When participants are encouraged to set their own goals for learning and their involvement is self-directed, a wider variety of goals can be met. For this reason it is important to allow for differences in goals and to encourage diverse participants appropriately (Hiemstra & Sisco, 1990). The opportunity for individually appropriate encouragement is, of course, dependent upon multidirectional communication.

➤ *As a workshop facilitator, what can you do to provide encouragement? What can*
a workshop facilitator do that might discourage participants?

Beginning the Workshop

At the beginning of a workshop, you have several overlapping tasks to accomplish as a director. You want to establish rapport with the participants, let the participants know what to expect, capture their attention, and create an environment that is conducive to learning. In this section, we present six different behaviors you can use to start a workshop. However, our expectation is that most workshops will not address all six of these components. For example, in a brief workshop with a familiar or cooperative group, it may not be necessary to identify goals, ground rules, and assumptions as distinct entities; all of these could be covered in a few sentences during a 5-minute overview. In a longer or more difficult workshop, it may be important to spend more time introducing the workshop with goals and objectives, ground rules, and assumptions as separate concerns. Depending on the particular workshop you are presenting, you will need to decide which of these components are the most important to create the intended learning environment and to encourage appropriate interaction patterns.

Introduction and Welcome

Presenter Introduction

In some workshops, a group leader or supervisor will introduce you as the presenter. In other situations you will introduce yourself. Introductions by others tend to be more formal than self-introductions. The introduction is a way to establish your credibility, which is a combination of perceived expertise and similarity. An example introduction that stresses expertise might sound something like, "In academic circles, Dr. Thompson is known for studying adolescent development for the past 15 years and has written 10 journal articles on the subject." In contrast, similarity has to do with participants' ability to relate to you as a person and to perceive common ground. Using the same example, an introduction that emphasizes similarity might also include, "Dr. Thompson is also the mother of two adolescent daughters and personally knows about the day-to-day stresses of parenting teenagers." Ideally, your introduction will establish your credibility related to both expertise and similarity. When preparing to be introduced or to introduce yourself, you should consider both, "What expertise, knowledge, or credentials do I have that should be highlighted to help participants trust in what I teach?" and, "What do I have in common with the participants that should be shared so they will trust me personally?"

In addition to establishing your credibility, it is important for you to share why you are interested in this particular workshop topic and group of participants. This builds another bridge between you and the subject matter and between you and the participants. For example, "I like presenting about stress management because I have always tended to be anxious, and the strategies and techniques that we will talk about are ones that I use every day" or, "I am particularly excited about presenting this material to high school teachers because I taught high school in this state for 10 years." Communicating your passion and commitment can excite the interest of the audience and begin to create a relationship between yourself and the participants.

➤ *What kind of information would you like to share in your workshops that will help participants connect with you personally and see you as a credible presenter?*

Participant Introductions

After you have introduced yourself to the workshop group, it may be appropriate to have participants introduce themselves. In a small group, it may be possible to go around the room and have each participant introduce himself or herself. Introductions often include participants' names, some background information, their position in the group or relationship to the other participants (e.g., supervisor, fellow student, support staff), and their interest in the current topic or a learning goal. If appropriate, you may want to build rapport by asking participants to share one thing about themselves that is unrelated to the workshop setting. For example, you can ask participants to share one thing about which they feel passionately. Responses to such an open question can vary as widely as, "Mountain biking," "Spending time with my kids," or "Growing vegetables in my garden." Should you choose to have participants introduce themselves, also consider the objectives of the workshop when deciding on the type of introduction. For instance, in a time management workshop, introductions could consist of name, position in the company, and "One way I waste time is . . ."

In a large group, it may not be practical to have all participants introduce themselves. However, there are some things you can do to get some of the same information or to establish some of the same group rapport. You can do a quick survey and have people stand or raise their hands to indicate their background: "How many of you here are managers? . . . technical staff? . . . clerical staff?" You can also ask a few participants to share goals or interests related to the workshop topic and ask for a show of hands to see if these interests are representative of the entire group. In order for participants to feel some connection with other participants in a large group, you can ask them to pair off or gather in small groups to share names, background, and interests within the workshop.

➤ *Will it be appropriate for participants to introduce themselves in your workshops? What kinds of introductions could you facilitate?*

Overview of the Workshop

It is usually helpful to give a brief overview of the workshop so that participants will know what to expect and mentally prepare for the types of learning involved. You may include your expectations as well as the outcomes desired by the requester. By letting people know that participation will be experiential, you can allow them to prepare for interactive learning. You also may want to have a written agenda or outline so that participants can see the progression of learning as it unfolds. Don't forget to plan breaks and let participants know when they're planned. Putting exact times on an agenda may not be a good idea because participants will know if you are running late and this may allow you less flexibility to improvise or adapt to changing circumstances.

Goals and Objectives

Presenting the goals and objectives of the workshop is a popular way to begin a workshop. You may not need to present both an outline and the goals and objectives because the information is often so similar. A set of goals and objectives can serve as an outline. If this is the case, learning activities should be organized in the same order as the goals and objectives are presented. Presenting your objectives will help give participants a concrete idea of what they will learn and what skills they will acquire.

These objectives also can be reviewed at the end of a workshop in order to highlight and consolidate learning.

Clarifying Expectations

At the beginning of a workshop, let participants know what to expect and give them an idea of behavior that is appropriate within the workshop environment. This is a vital step because the way you want participants to act and interact in a workshop may be very different than how they are expected to act in other learning, work, or social environments. Drum and Lawler (1988) suggested that clarifying participant roles was an essential aspect of creating a safe environment for self-exploration. They suggested that clarification of roles was necessary to reduce anxiety to a point where learning can occur at an optimal level. "Describing the anticipated style of interactions will encourage quicker and fuller involvement. . . . Pointing out the challenges they are likely to face—giving and receiving feedback, role-playing, risk taking, and disclosing—allows members to prepare for and accept them" (pp. 74-75). Therefore, if you want people to participate actively and to communicate interactively in your workshop, it is important to describe this kind of behavior at the outset.

Setting Ground Rules

A more specific way to clarify participant roles is to suggest ground rules that govern the way participants will interact. Ground rules or group norms are particularly helpful in structuring the environment for participants who are unfamiliar with workshop learning. Such behavioral guidelines can encourage appropriate learning and interactive behavior and discourage inappropriate and potentially disruptive behavior. If there is the possibility of disruptive behavior or active resistance to the ideas or activities presented in the workshop, you can set up ground rules that allow you to exercise more control or to structure the interactions in ways that prevent problems by predicting them. For example, if you are afraid that a few members may dominate the conversation, you can set up the expectation that, "Everyone will get a chance to speak once before any single individual speaks a second time." Ground rules like these are much easier to establish ahead of time than they are to suggest in the heat of a conflict. If you want people to raise their hand before speaking or to save their questions until the end of a lecturette, it is important to communicate these norms. Some matters of common respect like asking that only one person speak at a time and that all opinions should be given equal weight also may be clarified as ground rules. Some sample ground rules are summarized in Exhibit 6.3.

Clarifying Assumptions

At the beginning of a workshop, you might want to clarify your assumptions or to share the principles that are guiding you and the content and design of the workshop. Clarifying assumptions is particularly important when you are dealing with a controversial topic about which there may be some disagreement. For example, one of us recently presented a series of workshops on sexual orientation for a group of teachers with the assumption that gay, lesbian, and bisexual students are "at risk" and that teachers should be supportive of these students. During the first presentation, this assumption was not presented up front and participants asked a variety of questions throughout the entire workshop that were really about "where the facilitator was coming from." Because the workshop had not started with these assumptions, the questions often came up at inconvenient times that served to distract from the content and interrupt the pacing. When the workshop was presented again a few weeks later, these disruptions were avoided by clarifying assumptions at the outset.

➤ *What do you think are the important parts in providing an overview of a workshop? How can you present goals and objectives, clarify expectations, set ground rules, and/or clarify assumptions?*

Maintaining a Coherent Workshop Message

Chapter 4 addresses the importance of choosing a consistent theme. An important part of the directing role is using the theme in a way that helps the workshop fit together as a consistent and coherent package. Participants need to see and feel that sense of consistency. Referring back to a consistent theme at times of transition and reinforcing the theme with punch lines (see Chapter 7) are ways that make the activities fit together as a package and reinforce the most important concepts. Revisiting a theme is another way

EXHIBIT 6.3
Sample Workshop Ground Rules

Before anyone can speak a second time, everyone should have the opportunity to speak once.

All opinions must be considered and respected.

No interrupting each other.

Only one person may speak at a time.

The facilitator is the final judge (particularly in game-like activities).

It is possible to agree to disagree.

No put-downs, name calling, or personal attacks.

---

to organize previews and summaries by following the public speaking axiom that you should, "Tell them what you're going to tell them; tell them; and then tell them what you've told them."

➤ *What are some ways that you can use a theme to give your participants a consistent learning experience?*

Pacing and Timing

It has been said that any journey begins with a single step, and we can extend that metaphor to say that journeys of any length can be thought of as a series of several steps. The same is true of a workshop. The model presented here already provides one way to think of smaller workshop "steps" corresponding to different types of learning activities. Breaking learning into smaller pieces according to experiential learning processes also allows you to provide variety and to avoid the mistake of spending too much time on assimilation or traditional didactic presentation of information. As you decide how to pace and time your workshop activities, consider which of your goals are most important and allot your time according to these priorities. If the acquisition of new skills is essential, make sure you spend sufficient time on experimenting activities that emphasize practical skill building. If making changes in behavior "back home" is vital, ensure that there is enough time to plan for application to increase the likelihood of transfer of learning.

Another way to think about timing is in terms of what time of day the workshop will be offered and which sections of the workshop will correspond to which time periods. Make sure that you have enough time to facilitate each section of the entire workshop. However, it is also crucial to think about the impact of other daily, monthly, or annual events on your workshop. For instance, many of us can remember times when we've had to struggle to pay attention at about 1:30 p.m. in a day-long workshop. As a workshop facilitator, you may want to avoid scheduling the less active parts of a workshop during a predicted slow or sleepy time like this. You also should think twice about facilitating an information-laden workshop the afternoon before the company holiday party or at the same time as another major event. We have both inadvertently scheduled exciting workshops when other important events were going on. Regardless of the potential interest in those topics, we have learned the hard way not to compete with major rock concerts or university sporting events.

➤ *Do you need to improve your timing and pacing skills? What are some of the most relevant timing and pacing issues for the workshops you present?*

Concluding the Workshop

Reviewing Content to Consolidate Learning

At the end of a workshop, you will review what the participants have learned. This type of review serves two purposes. First, the review serves to reinforce what has already been learned. Second, it provides a connection between the beginning of a workshop when learning objectives were set and the end of a workshop when content is reviewed.

Planning for the Future

Planning for application is the final quadrant in the experiential learning cycle, and it should be included in every workshop. If you have included learning activities from all four experiential learning quadrants, then you can review learning by emphasizing this cycle of learning. Chapter 5 lists several activities that help participants plan for the future at the end of the workshop to ensure that transfer of learning takes place.

Feedback/Evaluations

There are several approaches to evaluation to consider. We discuss these strategies in Chapter 8. Feedback and evaluation usually occur at the end of a workshop, and asking for verbal feedback is often a useful way to conclude a workshop. Questions that serve the dual purpose of eliciting feedback and encouraging closure include, "What was the most important thing you gained from this workshop?" or, "Are there things that you wanted to learn about that we were not able to address today?" You might ask requesters if they have seen an increase in participant skills, both right after the workshop and some time after.

Follow-Up

After the workshop you may want to follow up with the workshop requester or with participants. Make sure that you keep any promises you made during the workshop, such as looking up a reference or sending someone extra handouts. If you have an ongoing relationship with the workshop requester or participants, it may be appropriate to check in after the workshop to see how it has impacted the participants.

➤ *What do you think are the most important things to do at the end of a workshop?*

Summary

This chapter outlined the events that occur in a typical workshop and discussed the role of directing these events. We suggested ways to create a positive learning environment and to begin a workshop effectively, maintain a consistent and coherent message, pace learning, and conclude the workshop. It is important to continue to think about these elements of structure and direction as you consider the complex and more subtle role of facilitation that is discussed in Chapter 7.

Planning for Application

1. When you think about workshops you will present in the future, which
   of the following elements do you think it is most important to include
   at the beginning of a workshop? Why?

   a. Introducing Self and Participants

   _____

   b. Overview of the Workshop

   _____

   c. Goals and Objectives

   _____

   d. Clarifying Expectations

   _____

   e. Setting Ground Rules

   _____

   f. Clarifying Assumptions

   _____

2. What can you do to maintain a coherent message in future workshops?
   For topics that you anticipate presenting in the future, can you identify
   a consistent theme that would help organize the workshop?

   _____

3. How can you end a workshop in a way that reinforces learning and
   helps participants plan for the future?

   _____

Facilitation Skills for Different Types of Experiential Learning

M ost human endeavors require complex sequences of behaviors that we regularly perform without conscious awareness. However, when learning a new activity, we frequently have to go back to square one and learn individual skills step by step. For example, a whitewater kayaker needs to learn to perform an "Eskimo roll" to right the kayak if it tips over in the middle of a rapid. To execute this complicated maneuver, a kayaker has to learn to perform a series of five discrete skills while hanging upside down underwater. An Eskimo roll requires that you tuck your body forward, position the paddle on the surface of the water alongside the kayak, sweep the paddle perpendicular to the boat, and draw the paddle toward you while snapping your hips into an upright position. To learn to roll, a kayaker needs to practice each of these five skills one at a time until they all fit together. With practice, the roll becomes automatic and the kayaker is unaware of performing all five skills; an Eskimo roll becomes one behavior rather than five.

Workshop facilitation is also an enterprise that involves learning and practicing a complex array of skills until they flow together naturally. We have broken down the elaborate endeavor of workshop facilitation into a few dozen skills that are frequently used by experienced facilitators. The process of dividing complex behaviors into discrete skills so that they can be identified, described, learned, and practiced is referred to as a "microskills" approach and previously has been applied to teaching (Allen & Ryan, 1969) and counseling (Ivey, 1971; Ivey & Authier, 1978).

In addition to planning activities and fine tuning your workshop design, what you, the facilitator, do and say in the workshop is of crucial importance. In other words, your behavior in the workshop can be looked at as another essential tool with which you can facilitate learning. This may not seem very earth-shattering—of course what facilitators do is important! However, being consciously aware of using both facilitation skills and learning activities to encourage all four types of experiential learning will make you a more confident and successful workshop facilitator.

In Chapter 5, we discuss learning activities, or what you encourage participants to do in the context of a workshop. The distinction between skills and activities is that facilitation skills are what YOU do; learning activities are what THEY do. This may seem like a rather fine distinction in some cases. It is true that many activities could be redefined as skills and vice versa.

For instance, you can have workshop participants listen to a lecture (a learning activity) or you can give a lecture (a facilitation skill). Throughout much of a workshop, facilitation and learning activities take place simultaneously. Learning activities are constructed using facilitation skills as a primary building material. We will try to avoid splitting hairs about the distinction between skills and activities and simply focus on facilitator behaviors in this chapter.

Assessing Your Facilitation Skills

As a way to introduce a few facilitation skills and briefly assess your preferences, please take a moment to take the following quiz. A scoring key is provided at the end. For each numbered item, use the following scale to indicate the likelihood that you would use a facilitation skill like the one listed.

4 = I am most likely to do/say this in my workshops.
3 = I am somewhat likely to do/say this in my workshops.
2 = I am less likely to do/say this in my workshops.
1 = I am least likely to do/say this in my workshops.

Reminders: Larger numbers indicate increased likelihood that you will use this skill. You should use all four rankings (1-4) in each numbered item.

1. a._____ Share your outline or agenda with the group.
   b._____ Use case studies.
   c._____ Ask for volunteers.
   d._____ Assign/suggest homework.
2. a._____ "We are doing this exercise because . . ."
   b._____ Take a vote.
   c._____ Use worksheets.
   d._____ "Let's spend some time as a group brainstorming ways that we will act differently from now on."
3. a._____ "Can you tell me more about your experience with that issue?"
   b._____ Provide informative handouts.
   c._____ "It seems that there is a disagreement within the group . . ."
   d._____ Encourage goal setting related to the program topic.
4. a._____ Use guided imagery to begin a program.
   b._____ Give lecturettes on the topic.
   c._____ Involve participants in role plays.
   d._____ "I'd like each of you to think about how you might use this new knowledge . . ."
5. a._____ Use brainstorming activities.
   b._____ Show videos.
   c._____ Ask participants to repeat a task, incorporating newly learned skills.
   d._____ "How will you now respond to (e.g.) racist comments?"
6. a._____ Set ground rules for the presentation.
   b._____ Answer participants' questions.
   c._____ Encourage direct interaction among the participants.
   d._____ Disclose how you have used the information in your own life.
7. a._____ "That's a great question. Does anyone have an answer for that one?"
   b._____ Identify themes in a group discussion.
   c._____ Ask for feedback regarding an exercise.
   d._____ Encourage future action related to the program topic.

Scoring: Write the number of points for each category and total.

1. a = _____ b = _____ c = _____ d = _____
2. a = _____ b = _____ c = _____ d = _____
3. a = _____ b = _____ c = _____ d = _____
4. a = _____ b = _____ c = _____ d = _____
5. a = _____ b = _____ c = _____ d = _____
6. a = _____ b = _____ c = _____ d = _____
7. a = _____ b = _____ c = _____ d = _____

Total: a = _____ b = _____ c = _____ d = _____

The highest numbers correspond to the skills you use most often; the lower numbers, less often.

"a" items refer to **engaging** *facilitation skills*
"b" items refer to **informing** *facilitation skills*
"c" items refer to **involving** *facilitation skills*
"d" items refer to **applying** *facilitation skills*

The next section will define and describe these different types of skills.

Four Types of Facilitation Skills

We have organized facilitation skills into four quadrants that correspond to four learning styles, the same way that learning activities were categorized. This correspondence between facilitation skills and learning styles is illustrated in Figure 7.1. We refer to these facilitation skills as engaging, informing, involving, and applying skills. We recommend using all four types of facilitation skills for the same reason that we advocate including all four types of learning activities; you can meet the primary learning needs of each participant, as well as encourage all participants to complete the experiential learning cycle. These four types of facilitation skills will be described next.

Engaging Facilitation Skills

Engaging facilitation skills are used to invite workshop participants to be fully engaged and actively involved in the workshop learning environment. Engaging skills help workshop participants reflect on their own experience and prepare them for interactive learning. These skills are used to activate knowledge that participants already possess and to get them motivated and interested in the topic. Engaging skills are employed to create curiosity and energy for learning. They help create personal meaning and encourage interpersonal connections. Engaging skills build bridges between participants' past experience and the current learning experience. Engaging facilitation skills most closely correspond to the needs of Imaginative Learners and are often used in reflecting activities.

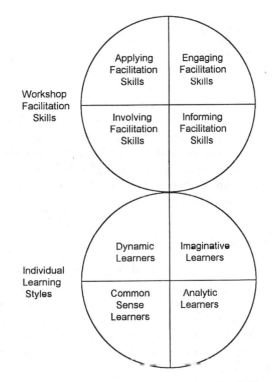

Figure 7.1. Correspondence Between Workshop Facilitation Skills and Individual Learning Styles

Informing Facilitation Skills

Informing facilitation skills help participants learn new information and conceptualize their own observations. Informing includes teaching factual information and allowing participants to gain new knowledge. Informing skills involve both content information from outside the group and process information about the group itself. Content information is frequently presented in a lecture format and includes facts, statistics, and theories. In contrast, process information can be collected in the form of surveys, sorting exercises, and other within-group activities. Once information is assimilated, these facilitation skills can be used to encourage participants to use the concepts to understand their own experience. Informing facilitation skills best meet the needs of Analytic Learners and correspond most closely to assimilating activities.

Involving Facilitation Skills

Involving facilitation skills create an opportunity for active experimentation with new knowledge and skills, encourage learning by practice, and allow participants to use the knowledge that has been gained in the workshop. Involving skills often are used to increase interpersonal interaction among participants. Because this type of learning occurs when the participants themselves practice new skills and gain hands-on experience, these facilitation skills require a shift in focus away from the facilitator and toward the group and its members. Involving facilitation skills correspond most closely with the needs of Common Sense Learners and are most often used in experimenting activities.

Applying Facilitation Skills

Applying facilitation skills allow participants to personalize their new learning by planning to apply the knowledge to their own personal or professional lives. Applying skills are used to build bridges between the workshop environment and "real life" outside the workshop, meet the needs of Dynamic Learners, and correspond most closely to planning activities. Characteristics of the four types of facilitation skills are summarized in Figure 7.2.

Your Facilitation Preferences

Now take a look back at your quiz scores. Is your use of facilitation skills distributed fairly evenly, or do you tend to use one or two types more frequently? Is there a category that you almost never use? These inequities can happen for several reasons. For example, some facilitators recognize that they tend to use the skills (and activities) that correspond with their own learning style—it simply seems a "better" and more effective way to teach people. Other differences in use of facilitation skills may come from the way facilitators were initially trained to do workshops. For instance, several facilitators have told us that it never occurred to them to encourage participants to use the knowledge at home. Also, issues of structure sometimes hamper facilitators from thinking about using certain types of skills—"I always go over my outline at the beginning, but how can I ask for reactions to a biology lab?" However, as common as it is to favor some

Figure 7.2. Characteristics of Workshop Facilitation Skills

types of skills and activities, we want to remind you that the use of all four types will facilitate the learning of all your participants.

Experimenting With Facilitation Skills

Now that you've read a description of the four types of facilitation skills, as well as some examples from the quiz, please answer the following questions:

1. You are aware that your workshop topic, gender differences, is emotionally loaded for many of the participants. What might you do or say at the beginning of the workshop to address this potential problem?

2. You want to make sure that your participants use the time management techniques they have learned after they leave the workshop. What might you do or say to encourage this?

---

3. About 10 minutes into the workshop, you are noticing the lack of voluntary participation, although it seems like most of the participants are interested and attentive. What might you do or say to encourage participation?

---

4. In a structured discussion about racial differences, you are aware that some participants have made inaccurate statements about the number of racial minority people in their particular setting. None of the participants have challenged these "data" and seem to be accepting the statements as fact. What do you do or say to address these inaccuracies?

Cofacilitation Skills

Many of us prefer to present workshops with another facilitator, particularly if the workshop is long or the topic is complex. The skills described in the catalog are all appropriate for cofacilitation. However, presenting a workshop with a colleague does require additional cofacilitation skills, which include planning, negotiating, sharing power, nonverbal communication, and patience. Prior planning is critical to almost any cofacilitator relationship. Cofacilitators should discuss the workshop outline and designate sections of the presentation in which each will take the lead. Otherwise, you may find yourself unprepared for part of the workshop, without the appropriate materials, or heading in different directions. It is also important for cofacilitators to discuss whether the division of leadership will be strict or if both feel comfortable "chiming in" when they have ideas to contribute. Nonverbal communication skills will help cofacilitators make decisions without stepping on one another's toes.

In addition to negotiating and planning which activities each cofacilitator will lead, it is also possible to adopt complementary roles. For instance, in a discussion designed to elicit potentially sensitive feelings, you may want to designate, ahead of time, who will play a supportive role and who will ask more challenging questions. Cofacilitation also allows presenters to utilize their personal strengths in terms of facilitation skills. One facilitator might be better at the involving, more experiential parts of a workshop whereas another might excel at preparing and delivering lecturettes. Whenever you work with a cofacilitator, it is important to be patient with and respectful of one another. By playing to the strengths of each facilitator, the workshop itself will be strengthened.

Examples of Facilitation Skills

Now that we've introduced the idea of facilitation skills and have given you some examples, we will share our catalog of facilitation skills. In the sections that follow, we will place each facilitation skill in the appropriate learning quadrant, define it, and give you some examples. As was the case in cataloging activities in Chapter 5, we have sorted skills into different categories, but this classification is not meant to be applied rigidly; many skills might facilitate more than one learning process. Facilitation skills can be used flexibly based on the desired outcome in the context of a particular workshop.

Examples of Engaging Facilitation Skills

Previewing Workshop Content or Goals

Previewing workshop content or goals involves sharing your outline or learning goals with the audience in order to increase motivation for learning.

Example: "We're going to be covering three main topics in this workshop. First, we'll talk about what being an ally for lesbian, gay, and bisexual people would mean. Then, we'll talk about why that might be important in your situation. Lastly, we'll explore how you could be an ally in your setting."

Setting Ground Rules or Group Norms

Setting ground rules or group norms (e.g., Yalom, 1985) clarifies your expectations for the workshop and helps to create a safe learning environment where participants will feel comfortable learning.

Example: "This program will involve some issues that many of us have strong feelings about. So, first of all, I'd like us to agree to listen to what each of us has to say and not interrupt one another . . ."

Example: "Because we can learn from each other during the course of this workshop, I'd like to set the ground rule that each person has the opportunity to speak once before anyone speaks twice . . ."

Reflecting

Reflecting what a participant has said (e.g., Corey, 1995; Ivey, 1988) makes the participant feel like he or she has been heard. Reflections usually focus on the affective or emotional part of what someone has said.

Example: "You seem to be excited about learning these new skills."

Example: "It makes you sad and frustrated to think about the gender inequities in your company."

Paraphrasing

Paraphrasing involves rewording what a participant has said (e.g., Corey, 1995; Ivey, 1988) in order to provide clarity. Paraphrasing usually focuses on the content of what the participant expresses.

Example: "It sounds like you were taught to avoid contact with people who were different from you."

Example: "So, your experience with time management techniques is that they are not very useful."

Reinforcing

Reinforcing is a way of encouraging or praising what has been said.

Example: "I'm glad you said that. I think that this is a particularly important distinction because . . ."

Example: "Excellent point! You've touched on what I think is a crucial issue when training new employees."

Asking for More Information

Asking for more information prompts participants to share more of their ideas with the workshop group

Example: "I'm not sure I understand. Can you tell me a little bit more?"

Example: "Can you say more about what leads you to that conclusion?"

Questioning

Questions (e.g., Corey, 1995; Ivey, 1988) require participants to respond to a specific stimulus and allow you to focus on a particular point or issue.

Example: "What are some ways that you think your own personal behavior is affected by stress?"

Example: "When you signed up for this workshop, what were the skills that you were hoping we would cover?"

Probing

Probing is a method of asking questions that encourages participants to look at their own ideas in a different way.

Example: "Where do you think you learned that message?"

Example: "How consistent is that with what you said earlier?"

Challenging Assumptions

Challenging assumptions questions the way participants have thought about a particular topic.

Example: "I guess I disagree. My experiences have been different. Could you tell me how you came to that conclusion?"

Example: "Hmm. . . I wonder if your discomfort with gay men might partially come from what you've heard from your family about gay people."

Bouncing Questions Back to the Group

Bouncing questions back to the group encourages thoughtful interaction and allows the facilitator to avoid answering a controversial question that may raise defensiveness. Participants are often more successfully challenged by one another than by the workshop facilitator.

Example: "That's a great question. Does anyone have an answer for that one?"

Example: "So, you think that some people may choose to remain in unhealthy situations. Does anyone have an idea why that might occur?"

Encouraging Brainstorming

Encouraging brainstorming allows participants to suggest a number of possibilities without criticism or evaluation.

Example: "Let's see how many ideas that we, as a group, can come up with that might solve this problem . . ."

Self-Disclosure That Increases Motivation

Self-disclosure that increases motivation can encourage learning by modeling an active learning approach.

Example: "Let me tell you why I think this is an important topic for us to discuss. In my experience, I have found that . . ."

Example: "When I first was learning how to be assertive, I too was worried that I was being 'mean.' What I realize now is that I can stand up for myself without stepping on others."

Examples of Informing Facilitation Skills

Clarifying Assumptions

Clarifying assumptions provides a contextual perspective on the information that will be shared.

Example: "The material I'll be presenting is based on a few assumptions that I'd like to clarify. First, I assume that women desire equal pay for equal work. Second, . . ."

Giving Information

Giving information is a straightforward presentation of factual or theoretical information. This can occur in a lecture format or in briefer statements of information.

Example: "It is estimated by the FBI that one out of every three women will be raped in her lifetime."

Surveying

Surveying is a way of collecting information from within the group itself by asking participants to indicate aspects of their own experience.

Example: "I'd like to see which learning styles are represented in this group. If your learning style is mostly imaginative, please stand up. . . . Next, please stand if your learning style is mostly analytic . . ."

Example: "Now, within your small groups, compare your answers. Are they mostly alike or different?"

Answering Questions

Answering questions involves providing information in response to a specific question or concern of a participant.

Example: "Good question. Generally there are two theories about why that occurs . . ."

Clarifying

Clarifying (e.g., Corey 1995) involves restating something that a participant has said and confirming whether there is an accurate understanding.

Example: "So, for you, the most important priority is . . . Is that right?"

Example: "Then, are you saying that you believe that sometimes a woman can prevent a sexual assault?"

Pointing Out What Was Not Mentioned

Pointing out what was not mentioned by the group is a way of providing information that may have been overlooked.

Example: "These are really good points about dating and marriage. However, I noticed that nobody talked about gay and lesbian relationships. Do you think the same patterns hold true for same-sex couples?"

Identifying Themes

Identifying themes gives the audience information about itself in the form of predominant patterns or ideas.

Example: "As I have heard the group discuss this idea, I'd like to point out the two ideas that came through most clearly to me. First, many of you feel that . . . Second, other people have had a different experience that suggests . . ."

Modeling New Behavior

Modeling new behavior (e.g., Corey, 1995) provides participants with observational information about how a particular behavior can occur. This modeling often precedes experimenting activities such as role-plays.

Example: "Let me demonstrate what I have been explaining. I'm going to act out a scene where I initiate a conversation with a stranger and try to get her to share information about herself."

Punch Lines

Punch lines are brief and memorable previews or summaries of important information. They are used to increase the likelihood that workshop content will be remembered.

Example: "If I wanted you to remember only one thing from this workshop, it would be, 'Differences aren't necessarily good or bad.' "

Example: "So, the most important points I want you to remember as you leave today are that, 'The facts are always helpful' and, 'That's why we should always seek more information.' "

Summarizing

Summarizing (e.g., Corey, 1995; Ivey, 1988) provides a brief review of information that has been presented.

Example: "Let me review the three main points of this part of the workshop . . ."

Example: "So far, we've discovered that each of us might do things that annoy or threaten our coworkers. For the next part of the workshop . . ."

Explaining

Explaining clarifies information that may be difficult for participants to understand.

Example: "Before we proceed, I want to tell you why I am sharing these ideas with you . . ."

Example: "As a way to introduce this next part, I'd like to go briefly over my understanding of why I was asked to speak to your group."

Self-Disclosure That Provides Information

Self-disclosure can be used to provide information in the form of the facilitator's personal experiences as related to the workshop topic.

Example: "As an example, I'll talk a little about what I have found to be true for myself . . ."

Examples of Involving Facilitation Skills

Prompting Participation

Prompting participation requires the facilitator to ask and/or encourage participants to do or say something in order to involve themselves in the workshop.

Example: "Who would like to volunteer for this role-play?"

Example: "Would anyone like to share what they wrote down?"

Encouraging New Behavior Within the Workshop

As people participate in workshop activities, it may be important to encourage them to experiment with new behavior that differs from their usual patterns. This skill is often used during role-plays or simulations.

Example: "How would you do it differently if you could? . . . Would you like to try it again and do some of those things?"

Example: "Let's try it differently this time. This time I want you to tell them exactly how you feel. Tell them what you really wish you could say but might be afraid to . . ."

Encouraging Direct Interaction/"Directing Traffic"

During some workshop activities, it may be important to encourage participants to interact directly with one another in new ways. This involvement can be made more safe or comfortable if the facilitator takes an active role in directing the interaction.

Example: "Why don't you go ahead and try saying that to someone else in the group and see if it feels comfortable."

Example: "Now, if someone said that to you, how would you react? . . . Can you go ahead and say that now?"

Connecting One Person's Ideas With Another's

During discussions or other activities, personal involvement and interaction can be increased if the facilitator actively points out similarities in participants' ideas or experiences.

Example: "That sounds a lot like the idea that Maria was expressing earlier. Did either of you notice that similarity?"

Example: "Actually, there is a common thread between what the two of you are saying, which is . . ."

Interpreting

Interpreting involves offering your ideas about potential explanations for why things happen or why a participant is acting, feeling, or behaving a certain way. Interpreting can give participants additional perspectives as well as encourage deeper self-exploration.

Example: "Given what you've said about your experiences with life feeling unpredictable, it makes sense to me that you're not so sure these time management techniques will work."

Example: (In response to a participant's question) "Why do people discriminate against others? Well, I think one part of the answer might lie in how those people feel about themselves."

Process Observation

Below the surface of what is said or done, many subtle processes occur. Making observational statements about the subtle interactions that a facilitator might notice can often have an impact on the group process itself (e.g., Yalom, 1985).

Example: "During the first part of our discussion, five different women have shared their ideas with the group and none of the men have said anything. Do you think it might be harder for men to talk about this topic?"

Example: "I've noticed that people were more eager to participate in the first half of the workshop as opposed to now. What do you think is happening to cause this?"

Immediacy

Immediacy is a way of addressing group interactions in the "here and now." It often involves self-disclosures or hunches that the facilitator may have about current group interactions or participants' feelings.

Example: "Let me tell you what I think is going on in the group right now. It seems like there are two pretty different ideas here, but I'm not sure if anyone has openly admitted that there is a conflict. How do you think we could address this difference?"

Asking for Feedback

In order to be responsive to participants, a facilitator can ask for direct feedback.

Example: "Before we continue with the second half of the workshop, I'd like to ask if there are things that I could do differently that would be more helpful."

Example: "Before we begin the afternoon session, I'd like to ask if there are any areas that you hoped I would cover that I haven't yet addressed?"

Encouraging Interpersonal Feedback

Participants are often more deeply impacted by feedback or information about themselves from other participants than they are by feedback from the facilitator. In order to increase involvement and interaction, facilitators can provide the opportunity for this feedback to be shared.

Example: "Do you have any feedback for Michael about what he said in this exercise? . . . Does anyone else have an idea for him about another approach that could have been taken?"

Example: In a role-play activity, set up the groups so that some participants will be actively role-playing, and others will be observers whose task will be to provide feedback.

Asking for Reactions to an Activity

In order to understand the impact of an activity, it may be important to process participants' reactions to the activity.

Examples: "What was it like to try something new?"
"Does anyone have any reactions they would like to share?"
"What were the feelings you had when watching that interaction?"

Focusing/Getting Back on Track

In order to maintain involvement with the workshop topic, it may be important to discourage irrelevant discussion and stay focused.

Example: "This is really interesting, but I'd like for us to return to the question that was asked earlier . . ."

Example: "It is really tempting to discuss campus politics, but let's get back to discussing what we can do in our own residence hall."

Examples of Applying Facilitation Skills

Encouraging New Behavior Outside the Workshop

As participants learn new skills within a workshop setting, it is often helpful to encourage them to experiment with new behavior outside the workshop.

Example: "Is this something that you could try to use in other parts of your life? For example, how would you be able to incorporate this into your work situation?"

Generalizing From One Environment to Another

Workshop participants may identify strengths and skills in one area that may be usefully applied to another area of their lives. Pointing out these strengths may be a helpful way to encourage someone to generalize a behavior from one area to another.

Example: "You have said that you feel comfortable meeting people at work but not in your personal life. Can you think of specific skills that you use at work that you could start to experiment with in other areas of your life?"

Exploring the Future

Focusing on future possibilities can help workshop participants foresee new opportunities for growth and change based on what they have learned in a workshop.

Example: "Let's think about how we might be able to use these skills and ideas in the future. Does anyone have an idea how we might use the material from the workshop today to plan for the future?"

Pointing Out Opportunities for Application

As participants talk about areas of struggle, a facilitator may be able to point out ways that workshop skills can be applied to solve a problem.

Example: "That sounds like a place where you might be able to try some of the strategies that we talked about today. How do you think you could adapt these ideas to that setting?"

Encouraging Action

It is often helpful to have participants share a particular plan of action at the end of a workshop in order to increase the likelihood that workshop learning will be applied.

Example: "As a result of what we have explored here today, I would like for each of you to think about changes that you would like to make in your own behavior. Let's jot down a few ideas in the form of an action plan and then we can share these plans with one another . . ."

Encouraging Goal Setting

Setting specific goals (e.g., Corey, 1995) is another way to encourage participants' application of workshop learning.

Example: "As a result of what you have learned today, please identify one way you would like to change your behavior. I would like for you to set a specific, measurable goal in this area and share it with someone else in the group."

Assigning Homework

Assigning homework can help get workshop participants to apply actively what they have learned in the workshop. Homework is particularly useful when used between sessions of a multisession workshop.

Example: "Before the next time we meet, I would like each of you to try to apply the things we have talked about. We will start next week by giving people a chance to report about what they tried and how it worked."

Brainstorming Solutions

Generating a creative list of different solutions to a particular problem is another way to encourage application.

Example: "That's an interesting problem. Let's see how many possible solutions we can generate as a group, and then you can select the ones that would work best for you . . ."

Self-Disclosure That Models Application

It may be appropriate for a facilitator to share ways that he or she has personally used similar learning as a way to model and encourage application.

Example: "I'd like to tell you a little bit about how I have applied this information in my own life."

Summary

This chapter focused on presenting and describing four types of facilitation skills—engaging, informing, involving, and applying skills. The types of skills and their uses in workshops were discussed as well as strategies for improving skills and working with a cofacilitator. Descriptions for specific skills of each type were provided along with examples.

Planning for Application

1. Go back to the quiz at the beginning of the chapter and take note of the one type of facilitation skill that you use least. List three or four specific skills within this quadrant, and identify ways that you could incorporate them in your upcoming workshops.

   _____

2. For the remaining three groups of facilitation skills, list at least one of each type to add to your repertoire.

   _____

3. In your next cofacilitated workshop, you and your cofacilitator can try using complementary skills or roles. For example, for one section of the workshop, one of you could present information while the other observes the group process. How can you divide roles with your cofacilitator during your next workshop?

Chapter

8

Workshop Evaluations

Strategies, Variables,
and Plans

Measuring your performance is more important in some situations than others. For instance, if you have just started jogging, you simply may want to go out and run until you're tired and then head for home. After a while, you may become curious and start to look at your watch at the beginning and end of your jog to know about how long you have run. If you decide to train for your first race, you might drive your car along your running route to measure a 10-kilometer course and buy a stopwatch to begin to keep track of your times. It may give you satisfaction to watch yourself improve your time for a 10K run. However, if you ever become a competitive athlete, the distance you run will be measured much more accurately and whether you win or lose a race may be a matter of only a few hundredths of a second. In each of these cases, the situation calls for different levels of measurement and a different method of evaluating your progress.

When any one of us sets out to achieve a goal, we use an evaluation process to determine if our goal has been accomplished. Evaluation can also be used to obtain information needed to help us improve our performances in the future. Four key questions related to workshop evaluations are addressed in this chapter. First, what is the purpose and who is the intended audience for your evaluation? Second, what kind of overall strategies should guide your evaluation? Third, what kind of variables should you measure? Fourth, what are the steps in planning an effective evaluation?

This chapter serves as a very brief introduction to the large field of program evaluation. In several of the sections, we refer to other resources. Many of the most useful books we have found are from the Program Evaluation Kit, edited by Joan L. Herman (1987). This set of nine concise books focuses on different aspects of the evaluation process. If your evaluation needs surpass what is addressed here, we recommend that you utilize some of the resources to which we refer.

Reflecting on Workshop Evaluation

1. What have you done to evaluate workshops or other programs in the past?

---

2. Are there other evaluation methods that you would be interested in using?

Why Should You Evaluate Your Workshops?

What is an evaluation and why should it be conducted? Lenning (1989) defines the evaluation process as "judgments about value, worth, and ways to improve" (p. 328) a program based on an assessment that involves collecting, transforming, and analyzing data. As you begin to plan a workshop evaluation, three questions should be answered. First, what is the purpose of the evaluation? Second, for whom is the evaluation being conducted? Third, who will conduct the evaluation? Once you clarify these three issues, you are prepared to choose an evaluation strategy, select your variables, and create an evaluation plan.

Purpose

Workshop evaluations can be used for many different purposes. Herman, Morris, and Fitz-Gibbon (1987) point out that evaluations can be used to answer a variety of questions, including, "To what extent is Program X meeting its goals?" "How can the program be improved?" and "Is Program X worth continuing or expanding?" The first step in considering an evaluation is to determine what question you are trying to answer. For example, in one situation you may want to conduct an evaluation simply to give you a rough idea of how you did and give you a few ideas for next time. At the other extreme is a situation in which workshop evaluations must demonstrate effectiveness in order to ensure your ongoing funding or employment. The type of evaluation you conduct will differ depending on its intended use.

Audience

Related to the question of the purpose of an evaluation is the intended audience. For whom is the evaluation being conducted? Who will see the results? How will this information be used? Depending on the context of the workshop you are providing, different stakeholders may have an interest in the results of your evaluations. Andrews (1997) pointed out that users of evaluative information may include individual learners or learner-interested second parties such as employers, program developers, administrators, and certifying and regulatory agencies. Herman et al. (1987) point out that "for some evaluations, of course, the roles of evaluator, sponsor, stakeholder, and user are all played by the same people" (p. 8). This is often the case in workshop evaluations. By clarifying the purpose and audience of these evaluations, you will be more prepared to make decisions about which strategies to employ.

Evaluator

Before you plan your evaluation, you must decide whether you should design and conduct the evaluation yourself or if you should select an outside evaluator. This decision will be impacted by the breadth and complexity of the evaluation question, your familiarity with the evaluation process, and the need for objectivity. Although many workshop presenters conduct their own evaluations, there may be situations that call for an outside evaluator who has more expertise or more time and resources to conduct an extensive evaluation. It may also be necessary to utilize an outside evaluator if you will be reporting your results to stakeholders or decision makers who may have concerns about your ability to evaluate your own workshop outcomes objectively. If you select an outside evaluator, you should choose someone who has experience and expertise appropriate to the evaluation being conducted.

➤ *What will be the purpose of your evaluations? Who will receive the results of the evaluation? How will this information be used? Will you conduct your own evaluation or will you select an outside evaluator?*

Choosing an Evaluation Strategy

Before developing a specific evaluation plan, a workshop evaluator must make three choices about evaluation strategies. First, will you use a formative or a summative strategy? Second, will you collect quantitative or qualitative data to evaluate your workshop? Third, will you be conducting a formal or an informal evaluation? These decisions will be based on the evaluation purpose and audience and will lay a foundation for choosing variables and developing a specific plan.

Formative or Summative Strategies

The first choice regarding an evaluation strategy is whether to conduct a summative or a formative evaluation (Herman et al., 1987; Lenning, 1989). A summative evaluation "looks at the total impact of a program" whereas a "formative evaluation requires collecting and sharing information for program improvement" (Morris & Fitz-Gibbon, 1978, pp. 8-9). In other words, a summative evaluation is most likely to occur at the end of a program and measure the outcome. A formative evaluation is more likely to occur in the midst of a workshop in order to improve it.

Summative evaluations at the conclusion of a workshop are most common because the short-term nature of a workshop makes it difficult to collect and use data for formative evaluations. Formative evaluations are possible if a workshop meets more than once and data can be collected and utilized between sessions. Or, if the same workshop is being presented to more than one group of participants, then evaluation data collected after early workshops can be used to shape subsequent presentations. This use of a formative evaluation strategy also provides the opportunity to see how different types of groups respond to the same material in order to improve your ability to adapt a workshop to a particular type of group. If a formative evaluation is to be used in the midst of a single-session workshop, it is most likely to be based on informal, qualitative feedback that is often collected verbally in order to make choices about workshop design based on participant preferences.

Quantitative or Qualitative Strategies

The second major choice regarding an evaluation strategy is whether to collect qualitative or quantitative data or both (Herman et al., 1987; Pietrzak, Ramler, Renner, Ford, & Gilbert, 1990). "Quantitative data give precise numerical measures, while qualitative data provide rich descriptive materials" (Caffarella, 1994, p. 136). Traditional methods of evaluation tended to emphasize the need for objective, quantitative data. However, more recent approaches to evaluation recognize the limitations of relying solely on numerical results and, therefore, also include qualitative measures. If your evaluations are simply for your own personal improvement, then you may find qualitative data more helpful. In contrast, if your evaluation will be used by administrators to make decisions about the worth and funding of your workshops, then it may be necessary to provide objective, quantitative measures of outcomes. Many workshop presenters choose to collect both qualitative and quantitative data to take advantage of the strengths of each strategy. Examples of qualitative evaluation questions are presented in Exhibit 8.1. These questions could be used in a formal, written evaluation or to generate informal, verbal feedback. The questions are worded in a way that suggests a summative strategy but could be adapted to be used in a formative evaluation ("What have you liked most about the workshop so far?" "How can the remainder of this workshop be improved to meet your needs better?"). Quantitative item examples are presented later in Exhibits 8.3 and 8.4, which highlight evaluation items related to satisfaction and the accomplishment of objectives.

Formal or Informal Strategies

The third choice you will make when choosing an evaluation strategy is whether to conduct a formal or informal evaluation. Stake (1967) made the distinction between informal evaluation that depends upon "casual observation, implicit goals, intuitive norms, and subjective judgment" (p. 523) and formal evaluation based on controlled comparisons and objective measures. In most workshop settings, it is helpful to conduct an ongoing

EXHIBIT 8.1
Examples of Qualitative Evaluation Questions

1. What did you like most about the workshop? Why?
2. What did you like least? Why?
3. Which workshop activity did you find most beneficial? Why?
4. Which activity was least helpful? Why?
5. What did the facilitator do to increase your ability or motivation to learn?
6. What did the facilitator do that may have decreased your ability or motivation to learn?
7. How could this workshop have been improved to better meet your needs?

---

informal evaluation even if a formal, summative evaluation is planned. Informal evaluation can be planned by providing time for feedback at choice points during the workshop or can occur spontaneously. Informal evaluation almost always takes the form of listening to feedback about your workshop and taking action on what you learn (Caffarella, 1994).

Combining Strategies

With three pairs of binary choices, there are eight possible combinations of evaluation strategies. However, some strategies are unlikely to be combined with others. For example, informal strategies are rarely quantitative (eliminating two possible combinations) and formative strategies in short-term programs are rarely formal (eliminating two more combinations). The remaining combinations represent four strategies that are commonly used to evaluate workshops. These four combinations of strategies and corresponding examples are presented in Exhibit 8.2.

➤ *What kinds of workshop evaluation strategies are you likely to employ? Formative or summative? Quantitative or qualitative? Formal or informal?*

Deciding Which Variables to Measure

Now that you have decided upon a combination of evaluation strategies, the next step is to determine what variables you want to measure or observe.

EXHIBIT 8.2
Four Combinations of Evaluation Strategies Commonly Used for Workshops

Strategies	Example
1. **Informal Qualitative Formative**	Half-way through a full-day workshop, the facilitator asks for verbal feedback and presents choices for how to spend time during the afternoon session.
2. **Informal Qualitative Summative**	At the end of a workshop, the facilitator leads a discussion about the learning activities used, including strengths and weaknesses of each activity. The facilitator takes notes and uses this feedback in designing her next workshop on the same topic (see Exhibit 8.1 for sample questions).
3. **Formal Quantitative Summative**	At the end of a workshop, the facilitator distributes an evaluation form that asks the participants to give numerical rankings regarding the accomplishment of each learning objective (see Exhibit 8.4 for sample questions).
4. **Formal Qualitative Summative**	At the end of a workshop, the facilitator distributes an evaluation form that asks participants to respond to open-ended questions about each of the learning activities (see Exhibit 8.1 for sample questions).

Most workshop evaluations attempt to answer the question, "How will recipients be different after receiving services?" (Pietrzak et al., 1990, p. 15). Most workshop evaluations target one of three types of variables; satisfaction, the accomplishment of learning objectives, or behavior change. The advantages and disadvantages of these variables are discussed in the following sections.

Evaluating Satisfaction

The easiest and most frequent target of workshop evaluation is satisfaction. Evaluating satisfaction answers the questions, "Were the participants satisfied with the workshop?" and "Did it meet their expectations?" This approach measures what Drum and Lawler (1988) refer to as "users'

EXHIBIT 8.3

Examples of Evaluation Items Measuring Satisfaction

Please respond to each of the statements below using the following scale:

1	*2*	*3*	*4*	*5*
strongly				*strongly*
disagree	*disagree*	*neutral*	*agree*	*agree*

1. The overall quality of this workshop was high.
2. This workshop met my expectations.
3. I learned a great deal of new information from this workshop.
4. The workshop effectively used a variety of activities to meet my learning needs.
5. The facilitator was responsive to the needs of participants.

perception of outcome." You are not directly measuring whether the participants actually changed their behavior after the workshop. It is often assumed that satisfaction is correlated with more important outcomes like learning or behavior change, but this is not necessarily true. Therefore, some writers caution against evaluating only satisfaction and encourage the evaluation of other outcomes (Cervero, 1984; Sork, 1997). Examples of evaluation items measuring satisfaction are presented in Exhibit 8.3. The evaluation items in this exhibit are most likely to be used in a formal, quantitative, summative evaluation strategy and could be used with almost any workshop topic.

Objective-Based Evaluation

The second type of evaluation variable is the learning objectives that were set by the presenter or in collaboration with the participants. "In most evaluations, you will want to measure or observe the extent to which goals have been achieved. You must make sure, however, that all the program's important objectives have been articulated" (Herman et al., 1987, p. 22). To evaluate the accomplishment of objectives, you should ask at least one question for each of the learning objectives. Examples of evaluation items measuring the accomplishment of objectives are presented in Exhibit 8.4. The sample items are based on a management skills workshop with four

EXHIBIT 8.4

Examples of Objective-Based Evaluation Items

Please respond to each of the statements below using the following scale:

1	*2*	*3*	*4*	*5*
strongly				*strongly*
disagree	*disagree*	*neutral*	*agree*	*agree*

1. I was encouraged to reflect on and use my own professional experience as a source of learning.
2. I learned at least three strategies for improving my effectiveness as a manager.
3. I had an opportunity to experiment actively with and practice at least one of these strategies.
4. I was encouraged to select behaviors and skills that would allow me to enact these strategies in my day-to-day life back in my work setting.

objectives based on four types of experiential learning and are most likely to be used in a formal, quantitative, and summative evaluation strategy.

The third type of evaluation variable is behavior change. Evaluating behavior change is often more difficult than evaluating satisfaction or objectives, but is a more stringent measure of whether a workshop actually made an impact. Behavior change can be evaluated either at the conclusion of a workshop or some time later. Behavior change can be rated by individual participants, by other participants in the workshop, by the facilitators, or by outside parties such as the participants' employer. Davis (1974) suggested that at the end of a workshop, participants can be asked to demonstrate the competencies that the workshop addressed and that the behavior can be rated to measure the success of the workshop.

Behavior change outside the workshop also can be used to evaluate outcome. Drum and Lawler (1988) suggested that workshop-related performance could be videotaped before and after a workshop and that this behavior could be rated by experts on criteria related to the workshop content. Job performance data before and after a job-related workshop also could serve as a method of evaluating behavior change outcome. Although this type of behavior-based evaluation is an attractive ideal, it is obvious that it would be difficult to use with a large group or with a workshop of short duration. In most cases, workshop facilitators will need to depend on evaluating satisfaction or participant perceptions of the accomplishment of objectives.

➤ *In your future workshop evaluations, do you plan to measure satisfaction, achievement of objectives, behavior change, or some other variables?*

Developing an Evaluation Plan

Pietrzak et al. (1990) emphasized the importance of carefully planning both how to implement your evaluation and how to utilize the results. An evaluation that is thoughtfully conducted but never used is not worth the time and effort required. Therefore, it is important to decide ahead of time how you will use the evaluation data and to build utilization into your evaluation plan. Kosecoff and Fink (1982) described an approach to evaluation defined by five sequential activities, which include formulating questions and standards, selecting a research design, collecting information, analyzing information, and reporting information. We use these five steps to address the process of developing an evaluation plan for workshops and will highlight the choices you need to make during each step.

Formulating Questions and Standards

The first step in developing an evaluation plan is to specify the question that the evaluation is intended to answer (Kosecoff & Fink, 1982; Pietrzak et al., 1990). Once again, it is important to consider the use of the evaluation and to get input from all the stakeholders who may be looking at the evaluation data and conclusions (Andrews, 1997; Pietrzak et al., 1990). Your evaluation question may be something like, "Will participants be more assertive in their communication after this workshop?" or, "Will there be a change in leadership strategies used and employees' perceptions of their managers as a result of this training?"

In addition to clarifying the evaluation question, you will need to decide how you will know whether the answer to the question is affirmative or negative. The answer addresses the issue of standards. Kosecoff and Fink (1982) defined setting evaluation standards as "deciding what kind of information will provide convincing evidence of a program's success" (p. 65). They also suggest basing evaluation standards on experts, past performance, comparisons with other groups or the same group at another time, norms, or the evaluator's program description (Kosecoff & Fink, 1982). For example, an evaluation that utilizes a comparison standard might hold as its criterion for success that there is a significant increase in scores on a particular measure between the beginning of the workshop and a point in time 2 weeks after the workshop.

➤ *What kind of questions are likely to guide your workshop evaluations?*

Selecting a Research Design

The second step in developing an evaluation plan is to select a research design (Herman et al., 1987; Kosecoff & Fink, 1982; Morris & Fitz-Gibbon, 1978). A research design "identifies when and from whom measurements will be taken and specifies the extent to which certain experimental controls will be used" (Pietrzak et al., 1990, p. 25). Two of the most fundamental questions regarding research designs are whether you will use repeated measures with the same group and whether a control group, which does not receive the "treatment," will be used. Most short-term workshops rely exclusively on a posttest-only design in which data are not collected before the workshop and a control group is not used. Although this method may be sufficient for some purposes, using this design makes it difficult to assess whether your workshop actually had an impact. If you use a pretest-posttest design, measuring the same group before and after a workshop, you can determine whether a change occurred. However, you cannot conclude that the workshop itself was responsible for the change; perhaps the change would have occurred anyway. In order to prove that the workshop caused the change, you must utilize a control group and demonstrate that change occurred in the experimental group (that participated in the workshop) but not in the control group (that did not participate). For more detailed information about research designs used in evaluation, we recommend *How to Design a Program Evaluation* by Fitz-Gibbon and Morris (1987a).

➤ *What kind of research design are you likely to use to evaluate your workshops? Will it be possible to use repeated measures or a control group?*

Collecting Information

The third step in planning an evaluation is deciding how to collect information related to the outcomes of your workshop. Possible information-collecting methods include observations, interviews, questionnaires, tests, product reviews, performance reviews, and portfolios (Caffarella, 1994). For evaluating workshops, written questionnaires are the most frequent method used for collecting information. Questionnaires are particularly useful for measuring satisfaction or the achievement of objectives. If you are trying to measure behavior change, you may have to use observations or performance reviews. If you use a questionnaire or a test, you have the choice of using a previously developed instrument, modifying an existing instrument, or developing a new instrument to fit your specific needs (Pietrzak et al., 1990). If you choose to use a previously developed instrument, you may be interested in the resources provided in *The Best Evaluations for Seminars and Conferences* published by the Learning Resources Network (1997) or the sample questionnaires in *Planning Programs for Adult Learners* by Caffarella (1994).

➤ *What method will you use to collect information? Will you design your own instrument or use one that already has been developed?*

Analyzing Information

The fourth step in planning an evaluation is deciding how to analyze your data (Kosecoff & Fink, 1982). If you have collected quantitative data, you will need to decide whether to use descriptive, correlational, or comparative statistics. "Descriptive statistics describe data in terms of measures of central tendency (mode, median, mode), variability (standard deviation and range), and frequency" (Kosecoff & Fink, 1982, p. 178). For example, what are the average performance ratings for employees who did and did not participate in a training workshop? Correlational statistics are used to determine the relationship between two or more variables. For example, are ratings of workshop satisfaction related to the number of years of schooling? Comparative statistics are used to determine if there is a significant difference between two or more scores. For example, is there a difference between pretest and posttest scores or between scores of the experimental and control groups that is unlikely to occur by chance? In addition to these methods for analyzing quantitative data, there are now increasingly sophisticated methods for analyzing qualitative data. For more detailed information on data analysis, we recommend *How to Analyze Data* by Fitz-Gibbon and Morris (1987b).

➤ *Are you most likely to use descriptive, correlational, or comparative statistics to analyze the results of a quantitative evaluation?*

Reporting Information

The final step in evaluation planning involves decisions about how to report the results of your evaluation (Kosccoff & Fink, 1982). Like other parts of the evaluation process, reporting results can vary in its degree of formality. An informal evaluation report may be a discussion of the workshop's strengths and weaknesses with the requester or a written summary of participants' comments. If you need to write a formal evaluation report, it will probably include the following sections: introduction, method, results, discussion, conclusions and recommendations, and an executive summary (Pietrzak et al., 1990). In addition to the written sections of the report, you should also consider ways to use tables and graphs to present data (Morris, Fitz-Gibbon, & Freeman, 1987). Your evaluation report should be a way for you to showcase what you have accomplished in your workshop. For more detailed information about writing evaluation reports, we recommend *How to Communicate Evaluation Findings* by Morris et al. (1987).

➤ *How will you present the results of your workshop evaluations? Will your evaluation report be informal or formal? Will you be able to use tables or graphs to present quantitative data?*

Summary

Four topics related to workshop evaluation were discussed in this chapter. First, the purposes and audiences for evaluation were presented. Second, three choices regarding evaluation strategies were highlighted. Third, the types of variables to be measured were explored. Finally, five steps in developing an evaluation plan were summarized.

Planning for Application

Think about the next workshop for which you will conduct an evaluation and answer the following questions, which relate to the issues presented in this chapter.

1. What is the purpose of the evaluation? Who will see and use the results?

_____

2. What strategies will be most useful for this evaluation? Formative or summative? Quantitative or qualitative? Formal or informal?

_____

3. What variables will you measure? Will you measure satisfaction, the achievement of objectives, behavior change, or some other variable?

_____

4. How will you specify your evaluation question? What standard will be used to determine success?

_____

5. How will you collect evaluation information? Will you use observation, questionnaires, tests, or some other method?

_____

6. How will you analyze your data? If you use quantitative data, will you use descriptive, correlational, or comparative statistics?

_____

7. How will you report your evaluation findings?

_____

Chapter

9

Improving Your Workshop Design, Directing, and Facilitation Skills

For most people reading this book, presenting a workshop is not a one-time occurrence. Many workshop facilitators have ongoing opportunities to refine and improve their skills and to experiment with different topics and activities. You can think about this process of improvement as similar to that of a competitive athlete who, over time, strives continually to fine tune her performance. In order to achieve this desired improvement, an athlete needs to reflect on her strengths, experiment with different approaches to training, and learn from other athletes and coaches. In a similar way, workshop presenters can identify areas for growth, try new things, and learn from others.

Consequently, this final chapter discusses the importance of reflecting upon your performance as a workshop presenter and planning for future improvement. We address ways to continue with your "training" in workshop design, directing, and facilitation skills, including collecting information, practicing new skills, and planning for the future. We describe general methods of improvement, as well as highlight issues unique to different sets of skills.

Reflecting on Your Workshop Skills

1. What are some of the skills related to designing workshops that you feel you have mastered? What are some of the design skills that you need to work on or add to your repertoire?

_____

2. What are some of the skills related to directing or structuring workshops that you feel are strengths? What are some of the direction skills that you need to learn or improve?

_____

3. What are some of the skills related to facilitating experiential learning that you feel you have mastered? What are some of the facilitation skills that you need to work on or add to your repertoire?

_____

Sources of Information

In addition to the formal evaluation methods highlighted in Chapter 8, there are other sources of feedback from which you can collect information that can help you improve your workshop skills. We will list some general sources of information in this section and then focus more on improving different types of workshop skills in the last three sections.

Self-Evaluation

Reflecting on your own performance may be one of the most important and reliable sources of feedback. Many of us have had the experience of facilitating workshops that went almost perfectly, as well as the experience of having that sinking feeling that things were falling apart after only about 10 minutes. Use your intuitive sense of what has gone well and what has not to identify your strengths and areas for growth. After a success or a "bomb," take the time to analyze what may have contributed to the outcome and what you may want to change next time. Was it the icebreaker, the way the workshop was advertised, where it was held, or how you facilitated the role-play? But don't be too hard on yourself. To paraphrase one of our former supervisors, "I've planned plenty of great workshops that nobody came to!"

Your Cofacilitator

If you are working with a cofacilitator, make sure you ask that person for feedback as well. In fact, it is a good idea to plan to have feedback meetings after each workshop that you cofacilitate. This might be just 10 minutes in the lobby of the building right after the workshop or you can set up a more formal meeting. Your cofacilitator is able to watch and evaluate your skills in a different way than the average participant, because your cofacilitator knows more about what was intended. In addition, providing regular feedback to your cofacilitator will help you continue to be aware of how activities and skills can be utilized and improved.

Ask a Peer to Observe

Another possibility is to ask an additional person to attend the workshop solely for the purpose of observing your performance. This may sound a bit intimidating, but since that person's undivided attention will be on you, it can also yield excellent feedback. You also can ask for the observer to focus on certain things, like a new skill or activity you are trying for the first time.

Ask for Feedback From the Requester

The requester is another good source of feedback, because you designed the workshop based on her or his recommendations. A frank discussion of whether the requesting group's needs were met, how this was accomplished, and what you could have done differently can result in valuable information for your continued improvement. In addition to helping you improve your general skills, this strategy also can augment your work in future workshops for that particular group. Exhibit 9.1 lists some questions you may want to ask yourself, your cofacilitator, or another observer.

EXHIBIT 9.1
Feedback Questions for Cofacilitators, Peers, or Requesters

What do you think went well in this workshop?
What did not go as well as you hoped?
Was the overall structure and design appropriate?
Was the learning environment positive?
Which activities did you think were most effective?
Which activities could be modified or improved?
What did I do well as a facilitator?
In what ways could my facilitation skills be improved?

Attend Other Workshops

Observing other workshop facilitators can give you insights that you can apply to your own work. As you observe others, take note of all aspects of their performances. With modification, you could utilize a list of reflection questions like the one provided in Exhibit 9.1 in order to structure your observation. For example, as you are observing you can be asking yourself, "What is going well in this workshop?" "What activities have been effective?" "How could this presenter improve her or his facilitation skills?" and "How can I adapt these ideas to use in my workshops?"

Improving Your Workshop Skills

How and what you choose to improve probably will be based on either the types of feedback you have received or the areas in which you wish to gain more expertise. If you have gathered information from the sources just described, you have probably identified some workshop skills that you wish to improve. The next sections provide several general ideas for skill improvement that you can adapt for your own needs.

So far, we have identified three sets of overlapping workshop skills: design skills, directing skills, and facilitation skills. As you may recall, design skills focus on the overall structure and sequence of the workshop and creating specific learning activities. Directing skills come into play as you create a comfortable learning environment and lead participants

EXHIBIT 9.2
Workshop Design Skills

Choosing an effective design strategy
Collecting useful information before the workshop
Setting appropriate goals and objectives
Identifying a consistent theme
Sequencing activities appropriately
Designing activities from all four learning quadrants
Balancing activities according to perceptual styles
Balancing activities according to personality types

---

through a coherent learning experience. Facilitation skills refer to specific behaviors in the workshop that encourage different types of learning. Although these skill categories are not mutually exclusive, we will discuss them separately to help you better identify areas for improvement.

Improving Your Workshop Design Skills

Reviewing Design Skills

In the four chapters related to designing workshops and learning activities (Chapters 2 through 5), numerous skills are identified. Because what we refer to as design skills were identified over several chapters, we will review eight of these design skills to help you identify your strengths and areas for improvement. The eight skills are listed in Exhibit 9.2. The first five skills relate to overall workshop design, whereas the last three are more closely related to selecting or designing specific learning activities.

The first design skill in our review is choosing an effective design strategy. This skill is introduced in Chapter 2 and involves deciding whether to measure the learning preferences of your group and match the design to these needs (measure-and-match strategy) or to offer a design that will meet the needs of all learners (something-for-everyone). Choosing either of these strategies also involves selecting a useful model, theory, or instrument to guide your design. If you are comfortable using either strategy with more than one conceptual model, this skill may be an area of strength. Otherwise, this may be a skill that you wish to target for improvement.

The next two skills are collecting useful information before the workshop and setting appropriate goals and objectives (both of these skills are introduced in Chapter 3). To consider your information-gathering skills, you may want to reflect on past workshops and decide whether the information you collected has been sufficient or if there are additional data you wish you had ahead of time. To contemplate your goal- and objective-setting skills, you may reflect on questions like whether your goals are generally too ambitious or not challenging enough, whether you tend to set too many or not enough objectives, and whether your objectives are clearly defined or too vague to be measured. Identifying areas for growth is the first step toward improving these skills.

The next two design skills in our review are identifying a consistent theme and sequencing activities appropriately (both of these skills are introduced in Chapter 4). Identifying a theme and using it to guide your design provides a sense of coherence and consistency. If you cannot identify the theme from your last workshop, this may be a skill to practice. When we introduced sequencing in Chapter 4, we suggest that following Kolb's (1984) cycle of learning is appropriate in many but not all workshops. If you can identify appropriate situations for alternate sequences, this skill may be a strength.

The last three skills we will review are related to selecting or designing learning activities that meet the needs of diverse learners. Chapter 5 addresses skills related to designing individual activities from all four learning quadrants. Are you equally comfortable designing reflecting, assimilating, experimenting, and planning activities? Or do you have activity-designing strengths that may be related to your own learning preferences? In Chapter 2, we introduce skills related to balancing learning activities according to perceptual styles and according to personality types. Can you design activities that appeal to auditory, visual, tactile, and kinesthetic learners? Or are there some perceptual needs that you should learn to address better? Are you able to balance your learning activities so that they meet the needs of extroverts and introverts, thinkers and feelers, and other needs based on personality type? Learning how to design diverse learning activities that can meet all of these needs is a complex skill that may take years to master.

In addition to considering the effectiveness of individual design skills, you can evaluate how the workshop went as a whole. Were participants able to complete the learning cycle? Were they provided enough information in

EXHIBIT 9.3
Rating Your Workshop Design Skills

For each of the design skills listed, rate yourself using the following scale:

A—strong skill; no improvement needed

B—pretty good; could use some refinement

C—definitely needs improvement

Design Skill	*Rating*
1. Choosing an effective design strategy	_____
2. Collecting useful information before the workshop	_____
3. Setting appropriate goals and objectives	_____
4. Identifying a consistent theme	_____
5. Sequencing activities appropriately	_____
6. Designing activities from all four learning quadrants	_____
7. Balancing activities according to perceptual styles	_____
8. Balancing activities according to personality types	_____

the assimilating activity to perform the experimenting activity? Should you add an additional reflecting activity between the two halves of the workshop?

Rating Your Workshop Design Skills

Now that we have reviewed skills related to designing workshops, we would like you to rate yourself on each of these eight skills. Exhibit 9.3 provides an opportunity to identify which skills you need to improve and which are already strong.

Experimenting With Design Skills

Based on the feedback you've received and the skills you are interested in developing, pick two or three skills to develop. For instance, you may decide to add an activity to your repertoire, improve your information gathering before the workshop, or pay better attention to your sequencing of activities. It is important to identify just a few areas for improvement at a time—it would be overwhelming to try to improve eight skills at once! Set a reasonable goal—like trying one new activity in each of your next few workshops—and do it. Make sure to stop, reflect, and gather feedback before you move on to incorporating more skills. The goal should not be simply to try many skills, but rather to do each skill well.

It is not unusual for workshop designers to prefer activities that complement their own personal styles and therefore to use these types of activities more often in their workshops. As you choose new activities to experiment and practice with, challenge yourself to add skills to your repertoire that do not correspond to your personal preferences. If you are primarily a Common Sense Learner, make sure that there are planning for application activities in your workshop "tool box." If you prefer to learn information by listening, push yourself to create an activity that involves tactile or kinesthetic learning. If you consider yourself extroverted, help yourself remember the importance of learning to use quieter activities that might appeal to introverts.

As you begin to try out new design skills, make sure that you also continue to gather feedback. Participant evaluations, feedback from your cofacilitator, and your intuitive sense of your growing skills will help you continue to refine your design skills. For instance, you may have mastered the mechanics of a fishbowl discussion (see Chapter 5), but you may not have a good sense yet of when a fishbowl works best.

Using New Design Skills

Next, we encourage you to be planful about using new activities and practice using other skills. It's great to learn about psychodrama, for instance, but if you never use that activity, then your time and energy have not been well utilized. Similarly, if you choose to target your sequencing skills, make this a focus of your next workshop design. As you choose which activities to learn and practice, you can also be thinking about where and when you might be able to use them. The example worksheet provided in Exhibit 9.4 may help you devise such a plan. Read the examples and then identify some skills you would like to try and designate opportunities for practice. Tools such as this worksheet (or ones you devise for yourself) can help guarantee that you are not only adding to your repertoire of skills, but that you are targeting appropriate skills for improvement as well as putting them to use.

EXHIBIT 9.4
Implementing New Design Skills

Desired New Skill/Activity	*Places I Can Use It*
Artwork	Career development workshop—have participants draw a "career time line"
Worksheets	Assertiveness workshop—have participants rate whether sample responses are assertive, passive, or aggressive
Sequencing activities	Review outline for next week's workshop!
_____	_____
_____	_____
_____	_____

Improving Your Workshop Directing Skills

Reviewing Directing Skills

The second broad set of workshop skills is those that focus on your role as a workshop director. Chapter 6 describes these skills in detail; we will list them in Exhibit 9.5 and briefly review them here. The first group of directing skills involves creating a positive learning environment. This set of skills includes arranging the physical environment, creating relationships between you and the participants as well as among the participants, facilitating multidirectional communication, building trust and acceptance, and providing encouragement. These skills reflect the learning climate or psychological "feel" of a workshop. Did your last workshop feel comfortable and open or was there tension in the air? Did participants interact smoothly with each other or was there a reluctance to speak? The answers to these types of questions can help you evaluate your current ability to create a positive learning environment.

The second set of directing skills takes us chronologically from the beginning to the end of a workshop. At the beginning, you must decide how to introduce yourself to the participants and how to introduce them to one another. How you introduce the workshop itself is equally crucial, in terms of providing an overview, sharing your goals and objectives, setting ground rules, and clarifying expectations and assumptions. In terms of the "flow" of the workshop, as a director you must maintain a consistent, understandable message as well as pay attention to pacing and timing. Lastly, you have choices about how to end the workshop. You may want to review the workshop content, assist participants in planning for the future, elicit feedback, or all three. Thinking about how your last workshop ran from start to finish may give you insight regarding this set of skills. Did you give participants the information they needed about your expectations in the beginning? Did you have enough time for all you wanted to accomplish? How did you end the workshop?

Rating Your Directing Skills

Now that we have reviewed workshop directing skills, you can use Exhibit 9.6 to rate yourself on each of these skills. This worksheet provides the chance to identify which skills are strong and which need to be improved.

Experimenting With Directing Skills

Again, we encourage you to use the information from your own reflection as well as from other sources to target areas for improvement. As you identify a few directing skills you want to add or improve, also think about how and when you will do so. Many directing considerations can be anticipated ahead of time, such as seating arrangements, introductions, and the ground rules you want to set. Some of your directing skills will need to be more spontaneous, however, such as when you discover that your room does not have movable chairs, or when attendance is much greater than expected and your plan for participant introductions will not work with such a large group.

Therefore, we encourage you to use two different planning strategies so you can anticipate the use of skills ahead of time as well as improve your

EXHIBIT 9.5
Workshop Directing Skills

Creating a positive learning environment
Arranging the physical environment
Creating relationships
Facilitating multidirectional communication
Building trust and acceptance
Providing encouragement

Beginning the workshop
Introductions and welcome
Overview
Goals and objectives
Clarifying expectations
Setting ground rules
Clarifying assumptions

Maintaining a coherent message

Pacing and timing

Concluding the workshop
Reviewing contents
Planning for the future
Feedback/Evaluations
Follow-up

---

ability to implement directing skills quickly when needed. First, for those directing skills that you can choose ahead of time, you can set up a worksheet like the one found in Exhibit 9.4, which encourages you to target specific skills for practice and mastery. Second, it might also make sense to do some brainstorming along the lines of "when this happens, I'll use this directing skill" for those more unpredictable moments. Exhibit 9.7 is provided for this purpose and will allow you to envision appropriate opportunities to use different directing skills. We encourage you to use the worksheets provided here as starting points but also to design your own worksheet formats that may more closely meet your individual needs.

EXHIBIT 9.6
Rating Your Workshop Directing Skills

For each of the directing skills listed, rate yourself using the following scale:

A—strong skill; no improvement needed
B—pretty good; could use some refinement
C—definitely needs improvement

Directing Skill	Rating
1. Creating a positive learning environment	___
a. Arranging the physical environment	___
b. Creating relationships	___
c. Multidirectional communication	___
d. Building trust and acceptance	___
e. Providing encouragement	___
2. Beginning the workshop	___
a. Introductions and welcome	___
b. Overview	___
c. Goals and objectives	___
d. Clarifying expectations	___
e. Setting ground rules	___
f. Clarifying assumptions	___
3. Maintaining a coherent message	___
4. Pacing and timing	___
5. Concluding the workshop	___
a. Reviewing contents	___
b. Planning for the future	___
c. Feedback/Evaluations	___
d. Follow-up	___

Improving Your Facilitation Skills

Reviewing Facilitation Skills

This section focuses on your facilitation skills—what you actually do in the workshop to encourage active learning. Chapter 7 includes a catalog

EXHIBIT 9.7
Implementing New Directing Skills

Problem in a previous workshop/ Skill I haven't mastered	*What I'll try differently next time*
Participants were worried I had a hidden agenda	Clarify my assumptions at the beginning
Workshop didn't have a clear end	Plan a specific closure activity
Participants weren't sure about credibility	Plan my introduction
_____	_____
_____	_____
_____	_____

listing 44 different facilitation skills. We will review the four basic types of facilitation skills here and then give you the opportunity to rate yourself on each of them as a way to plan for future improvement.

Engaging facilitation skills help participants become more actively involved in workshop learning by stimulating reflection on their own experiences. Engaging skills are often used at the beginning of a workshop or to facilitate a transition between sections of a workshop. Informing facilitation skills help participants form conceptualizations and learn new information. Involving facilitation skills encourage learning through hands-on practice and can increase communication among participants. Lastly, applying facilitation skills help participants prepare to utilize workshop learning "back home." Applying skills are often used at the end of a workshop to encourage transfer of learning.

Rating Your Facilitation Skills

Exhibits 9.8 through Exhibit 9.11 provide opportunities to rate your usage of 44 skills from four groups. Although this rating scale asks you to recognize strengths and weaknesses, there may also be skills that you never use. As we have mentioned previously, workshop facilitators sometimes

EXHIBIT 9.8
Rating Your Engaging Facilitation Skills

For each of the facilitation skills listed, rate yourself using the following scale:

A—strong skill; no improvement needed
B—pretty good; could use some refinement
C—definitely needs improvement

Engaging Facilitation Skill	*Rating*
1. Previewing Workshop Content or Goals	_____
2. Setting Ground Rules or Group Norms	_____
3. Reflecting	_____
4. Paraphrasing	_____
5. Reinforcing	_____
6. Asking for More Information	_____
7. Questions	_____
8. Probing	_____
9. Challenging Assumptions	_____
10. Bouncing Questions Back to the Group	_____
11. Encouraging Brainstorming	_____
12. Self-Disclosure that Increases Motivation	_____

lean too heavily on the skills that correspond to their own learning styles. Are there "holes" in your facilitation skill repertoire related to your own learning preferences?

In a general sense, facilitation skills are more about your behavior than are activities, so in evaluating and improving facilitation skills, make sure that the focus is on you. For instance, you may want to videotape yourself and then watch primarily your own behavior and how participants react to you, or you could ask yourself a list of questions focusing on your performance in the workshop.

You can use the reflection and data-gathering processes outlined above to identify skills to add to your set of workshop tools. For instance, if you recognize that you almost never use applying skills, we suggest that you turn to the catalog of skills in Chapter 7 and pick out one or two applying

EXHIBIT 9.9
Rating Your Informing Facilitation Skills

For each of the facilitation skills listed, rate yourself using the following scale:

A—strong skill; no improvement needed
B—pretty good; could use some refinement
C—definitely needs improvement

Informing Facilitation Skill	*Rating*
1. Clarifying Assumptions	_____
2. Giving Information	_____
3. Surveying	_____
4. Answering Questions	_____
5. Clarifying	_____
6. Pointing Out What Was Not Mentioned	_____
7. Identifying Themes	_____
8. Modeling New Behavior	_____
9. Punch Lines	_____
10. Summarizing	_____
11. Explaining	_____
12. Self-Disclosure That Provides Information	_____

skills with which to practice. Similarly, if you have realized that you do clarify assumptions, but only at the beginning of your workshops, we encourage you to think about other times during the course of a workshop you could use that skill and begin to experiment with those different times.

Experimenting With Facilitation Skills

We encourage you to consider thoughtfully all of your sources of feedback regarding your facilitation skills. Next, based on this information, pick a few facilitation skills and think about how you will use them in your upcoming workshops. It is sometimes more difficult to plan to use these skills in specific workshops, because often your use of facilitation skills is in response to participants' behavior rather than something you design

EXHIBIT 9.10

Rating Your Involving Facilitation Skills

For each of the facilitation skills listed, rate yourself using the following scale:

A—strong skill; no improvement needed
B—pretty good; could use some refinement
C—definitely needs improvement

Involving Facilitation Skill	*Rating*
1. Prompting Participation	_____
2. Encouraging New Behavior Within	_____
3. Encouraging Direct Interaction	_____
4. Connecting People's Ideas	_____
5. Interpreting	_____
6. Process Observation	_____
7. Immediacy	_____
8. Asking for Feedback	_____
9. Encouraging Interpersonal Feedback	_____
10. Asking for Reactions to an Activity	_____
11. Focusing/Getting Back on Track	_____

ahead of time. For instance, you will decide to bounce a question back to the participants (see Chapter 7) the moment the question is asked, not beforehand; or your decision to make a process observation (see Chapter 7) will stem from your observation of a particular group dynamic. So, as you target the new skills you want to incorporate into your facilitation tool bag, it may be more helpful to think of potential workshop situations and then choose appropriate facilitation skills. Exhibit 9.12 gives you an idea of how you might plan to use your new facilitation skills.

We encourage you to create a worksheet like this one to aid in your planning to use new facilitation skills. Especially since you may not be able to predict which workshops will require which skills, having thought about potential situations and corresponding skills will better allow you to recognize those situations when they do occur. This will help you increase your experimentation and use of the facilitation skills that you have identified.

EXHIBIT 9.11
Rating Your Applying Facilitation Skills

For each of the facilitation skills listed, rate yourself using the following scale:

A—strong skill; no improvement needed
B—pretty good; could use some refinement
C—definitely needs improvement

Applying Facilitation Skill	*Rating*
1. Encouraging New Behavior Outside	_____
2. Generalizing to Another Environment	_____
3. Exploring the Future	_____
4. Pointing Out Opportunities for Application	_____
5. Encouraging Action	_____
6. Encouraging Goal Setting	_____
7. Assigning Homework	_____
8. Brainstorming Solutions	_____
9. Self-Disclosure That Models Application	_____

Summary

This chapter discussed ways to improve workshop design, directing, and facilitation skills. Self-evaluation and reflection were emphasized, as was collecting feedback from multiple sources. Worksheets for rating current skills and ideas for targeting and implementing new skills were outlined.

Planning for Application

1. What are some specific questions you can ask, verbally or in writing, that will allow you to gather the type of information you need to plan for future improvement?

EXHIBIT 9.12

Implementing New Facilitation Skills

When this happens . . .	*I will try this skill . . .*
I sense that a participant has more to say	Ask for more information
I want the participants to generate ideas of their own	Brainstorming
I want to confirm or restate a participant's point	Clarify or Paraphrase
Participants seem to be talking only to me	Encourage direct interaction
I'm not sure of the impact of an activity on the participants	Ask for reactions
I want to help participants specifically apply the workshop knowledge	Encourage action or goal setting
_____	_____
_____	_____
_____	_____
_____	_____

2. What are some design skills you would like to learn and/or improve?

_____

3. What are some facilitation skills you would like to learn and/or improve?

_____

4. What are some directing skills you would like to learn and/or improve?

_____

5. How will you go about adding these skills to your repertoire?

_____

References

Abery, B. (1994). *Self-determination for youth with disabilities: A family education curriculum*. Minneapolis: University of Minnesota, Institute on Community Integration.

Allen, D., & Ryan, K. (1969). *Microteaching*. Reading, MA: Addison-Wesley.

Alvino, J. (1993). Teaching our children to solve "fuzzy" problems. *PTA Today, 18*(5), 13-14.

American Heritage dictionary of the English language (3rd ed.). (1992). New York: Houghton Mifflin.

Anderson, K. J. (1995). The use of a structured career development group to increase career identity: An exploratory study. *Journal of Career Development, 21*(4), 279-291.

Andrews, G. J. (1997). Workshop evaluation: Old myths and new wisdom. In J. A. Fleming (Ed.), *New directions for adult and continuing education: No. 76. New perspectives on designing and implementing effective workshops* (pp. 71-85). San Francisco: Jossey-Bass.

Angelo, T. A., & Cross, K. P. (1993). *Classroom assessment techniques: A handbook for college teachers* (2nd ed.). San Francisco: Jossey-Bass.

Belenky, M. F., Clinchy, B. M., Goldberger, N. R., & Tarule, J. M. (1986). *Women's way of knowing: The development of self, voice, and mind*. New York: Basic Books.

Berry, B. A., & Kaufman, R. (1994). Breaking the ice: Training 101. *Training and Development, 48*(2), 19-23.

Bertcher, H. J. (1988). *Staff development in human service organizations*. Englewood Cliffs, NJ: Prentice Hall.

Bourne, E. J. (1990). *The anxiety and phobia workbook*. New York: New Harbinger.

Boyce, B. A. (1995). The case study approach: Teaching about the gray areas. *Journal of Physical Education, Recreation & Dance, 66*(5), 43-47.

Brammer, L. (1992). *Coping with life transitions* (ERIC Clearinghouse on Counseling and Personnel Services Report No. ED350527).

Briggs, K. C., & Myers, I. B. (1988). *Myers-Briggs Type Indicator: Form G*. Palo Alto, CA: Consulting Psychologists Press.

Brock, C. S. (1991). Ethical development through student activities development. *Campus Activities Programming, 24*(6), 54-59.

Brookfield, S. D. (1990). *The skillful teacher*. San Francisco: Jossey-Bass.

Burstyn, J. (1993, April). *New tools for multicultural education: A response to Patricia Seed's "Multiculturalism and the predicament of the comparative method in historical and social science research and teaching."* Paper presented at the meeting of the American Educational Research Association, Atlanta, GA.

Caffarella, R. S. (1994). *Planning programs for adult learners: A practical guide for educators, trainers, and staff developers.* San Francisco: Jossey-Bass.

Cattaneo, M. (1994). Addressing culture and values in the training of art therapists. *Art Therapy: Journal of the American Art Therapy Association, 11*(3), 184-186.

Cervero, R. M. (1984). Evaluating workshop implementation and outcomes. In T. J. Sork (Ed.), *New directions for adult and continuing education: No. 22. Designing and implementing effective workshops* (pp. 55-67). San Francisco: Jossey-Bass.

Chapin, H. (1985). Cat's in the cradle. On *Anthology of Harry Chapin* [CD]. New York: Electra/Asylum. (Originally released in 1974)

Cooper, S., & Heenan, C. (1980). *Preparing, designing, leading workshops: A humanistic approach.* Boston: CBI.

Corey, G. (1995). *Theory and practice of group counseling* (4th ed.). Pacific Grove, CA: Brooks Cole.

Cougar, J. (1983). The authority song. On *American Fool.* [CD]. New York: Riva.

Crego, J., & Powell, J. (1996). Simulated environments for the exercising of critical decision makers: Utilizing networked multimedia. *Journal of Instruction Delivery Systems, 9*(2), 35-39.

Crookall, D., & Arai, K. (1995). *Simulation and gaming across disciplines and cultures: ISAGA at a watershed.* Thousand Oaks, CA: Sage.

Dahmer, B. (1992). Kinder, gentler icebreakers. *Training and Development, 46*(8), 46-49.

D'Arcy, J. (1992). *Technically speaking: Proven ways to make your next presentation a success.* New York: AMACOM.

Davis, L. N. (1974). *Planning, conducting, and evaluating workshops.* San Diego, CA: Pfeiffer & Company.

DeFrancisco, V. L. (1992). Ethnography and gender: Learning to talk like girls and boys. *Topics in Language Disorders, 12*(3), 40-53.

Dipboye, R. L. (1997). Organizational barriers to implementing a rational model of training. In M. A. Quinones & A. Ehrenstein (Eds.), *Training for a rapidly changing workplace* (pp. 31-60). Washington, DC: American Psychological Association.

Drum, D. J., & Lawler, A. C. (1988). *Developmental interventions: Theories, principles, and practices.* Columbus, OH: Merrill.

Dunn, R., & Dunn, K. (1993). *Teaching secondary students through their individual learning styles: Practical approaches for grades 7-12.* Boston: Allyn & Bacon.

Dunn, R., Dunn, K., & Price, G. E. (1986). *Productivity Environmental Preference Survey.* Lawrence, KS: Price Systems, Inc.

Dunn, R., Dunn, K., & Price, G. E. (1989). *Learning Style Inventory.* Lawrence, KS: Price Systems, Inc. (Original work published 1975)

Fitz-Gibbon, C. T., & Morris, L. L. (1987a). *How to analyze data* (Vol. 8 in J. L. Herman [Ed.], *Program evaluation kit*). Newbury Park, CA: Sage.

Fitz-Gibbon, C. T., & Morris, L. L. (1987b). *How to design a program evaluation* (Vol. 3 in J. L. Herman [Ed.], *Program evaluation kit*). Newbury Park, CA: Sage.

Fleming, J. A. (1997). Editor's notes. In J. A. Fleming (Ed.), *New directions for adult and continuing education: No. 76. New perspectives on designing and implementing effective workshops* (pp. 1-4). San Francisco: Jossey-Bass.

Gaw, K. F. (1996, March). *Sensitizing college personnel workers through simulation gaming.* Presented at the meeting of the American College Personnel Association, Baltimore, MD.

Gay, G. (1994). *A synthesis of scholarship in multicultural education* (Urban Monograph Series). Oak Brook, IL: North Central Regional Educational Laboratory.

Gmelch, W. H., & Chan, W. (1994). *Thriving on stress for success.* Thousand Oaks, CA: Corwin Press.

Golas, K. (1995). Computer-based English language training for the Royal Saudi Naval Forces. *Journal of Interactive Instruction Development, 7*(4), 3-9.

Hagar, S. (1984). I can't drive 55. On *VOA* [CD]. Los Angeles: Geffen.

Hentschel, D. (1997). Confessions of a workshop-aholic. In J. A. Fleming (Ed.), *New directions for adult and continuing education: No. 76. New perspectives on designing and implementing effective workshops* (pp. 87-94). San Francisco, CA: Jossey-Bass.

Herman, J. L. (Ed.). (1987). *Program evaluation kit* (Vols. 1-9). Newbury Park, CA: Sage.

Herman, J. L., Morris, L. L., & Fitz-Gibbon, C. T. (1987). *Evaluator's handbook* (2nd ed.), (Vol. 1 in J. L. Herman [Ed.], *Program evaluation kit*). Newbury Park, CA: Sage.

Hiemstra, R. (1991). Aspects of effective learning environments. In R. Hiemstra (Ed.), *New directions for adult and continuing education: No. 50. Creating environments for effective adult learning* (pp. 41-50). San Francisco: Jossey-Bass.

Hiemstra, R., & Sisco, B. (1990). *Individualizing instruction: Making learning personal, empowering, and successful.* San Francisco: Jossey-Bass.

Hoar, M. (1994, September). *Life histories and learning: Language, the self and education.* Paper presented at the Interdisciplinary Residential Conference, Brighton, England.

Ivey, A. E. (1971). *Microcounseling: Innovations in interviewing training.* Springfield, IL: Charles C Thomas.

Ivey, A. E. (1988). *Intentional interviewing and counseling: Facilitating client development* (2nd ed.) Belmont, CA: Brooks/Cole.

Ivey, A. E., & Authier, J. (1978). *Microcounseling: Innovations in interviewing, counseling, psychotherapy, and psychoeducation.* Springfield, IL: Charles C Thomas.

Jalali, F. (1988). A cross-cultural comparative analysis of the learning styles and field dependence/independence characteristics of selected fourth-, fifth-, and sixth-grade students of Afro, Chinese, Greek, and Mexican heritage (Doctoral dissertation, St. Johns University, Jamaica, NY, 1990). *Dissertation Abstracts International, 50*(62), 344A.

Janus, E. S. (1992). *Skills for diversity: Description, evaluation, and recommendations.* St. Paul, MN: William Mitchell College of Law.

Johnson-Bailey, J., & Cervero, R. M. (1997). Negotiating power dynamics in workshops. In J. A. Fleming (Ed.), *New directions for adult and continuing education: No. 76. New perspectives on designing and implementing effective workshops* (pp. 41-50). San Francisco, CA: Jossey-Bass.

Jung, C. G. (1971a). *Psychological types* (H. G. Baynes, Trans. Revised by R. F. C. Hull). (Vol. 6 of *The collected works of C. G. Jung*). Princeton, NJ: Princeton University Press. (Original work published 1921)

Jung, C. G. (1971b). *Psychological typology* (H. G. Baynes, Trans. Revised by R. F. C. Hull). (Vol. 6 of *The collected works of C. G. Jung*). Princeton, NJ: Princeton University Press. (Original work published 1936)

Knowles, M. S. (1980). *The modern practice of adult education: From pedagogy to andragogy* (Rev. ed.). New York: Cambridge University Press.

Knox, A. B. (1986). *Helping adults learn.* San Francisco: Jossey-Bass.

Kolb, D. A. (1984). *Experiential learning: Experience as the source of learning and development.* Englewood Cliffs, NJ: Prentice Hall.

Kolb, D. A. (1985). *Learning Styles Inventory* (rev.). Boston: McBer & Company.

Kolb, D. A., & Wolfe, D. M. (1981). *Professional education and career development: A cross-sectional study of adaptive competencies in experiential learning* (ERIC/Higher Education Research Report No. ED209 493/CE 030 519).

Kosecoff, J., & Fink, A. (1982). *Evaluation basics: A practitioner's manual.* Beverly Hills, CA: Sage.

Kraemer, B. (1996, March). *Meeting the needs of nontraditional students: Retention and transfer studies.* Paper presented at the Annual Meeting of the North Central Association, Chicago.

Kuhn, T. S. (1970). *The structure of scientific revolutions.* Chicago: University of Chicago Press.

Lambert, C. (1988). *The business presentations workbook.* Englewood Cliffs, NJ: Prentice Hall.

Learning Resources Network. (1997). *The best evaluations for seminars and conferences* (Learning Resources Network [LERN] Research Report No. 02-066). Manhattan, KS: Author.

Lenning, O. T. (1989). Assessment and evaluation. In U. Delworth & G. R. Hanson (Eds.), *Student services: A handbook for the profession* (pp. 327-352). San Francisco: Jossey-Bass.

LeRoy, M. (Producer), & Fleming, V. (Director). (1939). *The wizard of Oz* [Film]. Washington, DC: MGM/UA Home Video.

Loughary, J. W., & Hopson, B. (1979). *Producing workshops, seminars, and short courses: A trainer's handbook.* Chicago: Follett.

Marshall, J. C., Rice, L. L., & Cordts, J. (1986, April). *The experiential model of learning styles: A validity study.* Presented at the meeting of the American Educational Research Association, San Francisco.

McCarthy, B. (1980). *The 4MAT system: Teaching to learning styles with right/left mode techniques.* Arlington Heights, IL: EXCEL

McCarthy, B. (1990, October). Using the 4MAT system to bring learning styles to school. *Educational Leadership*, pp. 31-37.

Moreno, J. L. (1944). *Psychodrama: Collected papers.* New York: Beacon House.

Morgan, B., Holmes, G. E., & Bundy, C. E. (1963). *Methods in adult education* (2nd ed.). Danville, IL: Interstate Printers.

Morris, L. L., & Fitz-Gibbon, C. T. (1978). *Evaluator's handbook* (Vol. 1 in L. L. Morris [Ed.], *Program evaluation kit*). Beverly Hills, CA: Sage.

Morris, L. L., Fitz-Gibbon, C. T., & Freeman, M. E. (1987). *How to communicate evaluation findings* (Vol. 9 in J. L. Herman [Ed.], *Program evaluation kit*). Newbury Park, CA: Sage.

Morrisey, G. L., Sechrest, T. L., & Warman, W. B. (1997). *Loud and clear: How to prepare and deliver effective business and technical presentations.* Reading, MA: Addison-Wesley.

Myers, I. B., & McCaulley, M. H. (1985). *Manual: A guide to the development and use of the Myers-Briggs Type Indicator.* Palo Alto, CA: Consulting Psychologists Press.

Obear, K. (1991, March). *Training new leaders: Strategies to design and facilitate workshops.* Paper presented at the meeting of the American College Personnel Association, Atlanta, GA.

Onstenk, J. H. A. M. (1992). Skills needed in the workplace. In A. Tuijnman & M. Van de Kamp (Eds.), *Learning across the lifespan: Theories, research, policies*. London: Pergamon.

Onstenk, J. H. A. M. (1995). Human resources development and on-the-job learning. In M. Mulder, W. J. Nijhof, & R. O. Brinkerhoff (Eds.), *Corporate training for effective performance*. Boston, MA: Kluwer.

Palmer, A. B. (1981). Learning cycles: Models of behavioral change. *The 1981 annual handbook for group facilitators*. San Diego, CA: University Associates.

Pfeiffer, J. W. (1990). *Reference guide to handbooks and annuals*. San Diego, CA: Pfeiffer & Company.

Peoples, D. A. (1992). *Presentations plus: David Peoples' proven techniques*. New York: John Wiley.

Pietrzak, J., Ramler, M., Renner, T., Ford, L., & Gilbert, N. (1990). *Practical program evaluation: Examples from child abuse prevention*. Newbury Park, CA: Sage.

Priles, M. A. (1993). The fishbowl discussion: A strategy for large honors classes. *English Journal, 82*(6), 49-50.

Proudman, B. (1992). Experiential education as emotionally-engaged learning. *Journal of Experiential Education, 15*(2), 19-23.

Schaef, A. W. (1985). *Women's reality: How you can realize your full potential*. New York: HarperCollins.

Soriano, F. I. (1995). *Conducting needs assessments: A multidisciplinary approach*. Thousand Oaks, CA: Sage.

Sork, T. J. (1984). The workshop as a unique instructional format. In T. J. Sork (Ed.), *New directions for continuing education: No. 22. Designing and implementing effective workshops* (pp. 3-10). San Francisco: Jossey-Bass.

Sork, T. J. (1997). Workshop planning. In T. A. Fleming (Ed.), *New directions for adult and continuing education: No. 76. New perspectives on designing and implementing effective workshops* (pp. 5-17). San Francisco: Jossey-Bass.

Stake, R. E. (1967). The countenance of educational evaluation. *Teachers College Record, 68,* 523-540.

Stech, E., & Ratcliffe, S. A. (1977). *Working in groups: A communication manual for leaders and participants in task-oriented groups*. Skokie, IL: National Textbook.

Steinert, Y. (1993). Twelve tips for using role-plays in clinical training. *Medical Teacher, 15*(4), 283-291.

Stevens, C. (1970). Father and son. On *Tea for the Tillerman*. [CD]. Hollywood, CA: A & M.

Super, D. E. (1987). Career and life development. In D. Brown, L. Brooks, & Associates (Eds.), *Career choice and development*. San Francisco: Jossey-Bass.

Szczypkowski, R. (1980). Objectives and activities. In A. B. Knox (Ed.), *Developing, administering, and evaluating adult education*. San Francisco: Jossey-Bass.

Tannen, D. (1994). *Talking from 9 to 5: How women's and men's conversational styles affect who gets heard, who gets credit, and what gets done at work*. New York: William Morrow.

van Ments, M. (1992). Role-play without tears—Some problems of using role-play. *Simulation Games for Learning, 22*(2), 82-90.

Vasquez, J. (1990). Teaching to the distinctive traits of minority students. *The ERIC Clearing House, 63*(7), 299-304.

Vaught, B. C., Hoy, F., & Buchanan, W. W. (1985). *Employee development programs: An organizational approach*. Westport, CT: Quorum Books.

Vosko, R. S. (1991). Where we learn shapes our learning. In R. Hiemstra (Ed.), *New directions for adult and continuing education: No. 50. Creating environments for effective adult learning* (pp. 41-50). San Francisco: Jossey-Bass.

Witkin, B. R., & Altschuld, J. W. (1995). *Planning and conducting needs assessments: A practical guide.* Thousand Oaks, CA: Sage.

Wlodkowski, R. J. (1997). Motivation with a mission: Understanding motivation and culture in workshop design. In J. A. Fleming (Ed.), *New directions for adult and continuing education: No. 76. New perspectives on designing and implementing effective workshops* (pp. 19-31). San Francisco, CA: Jossey-Bass.

Yalom, I. D. (1985). *The theory and practice of group psychotherapy* (3rd ed.). New York: Basic Books.

Index

Activities. *See* Learning activities

Analytic learners. *See* Learning styles, four types

Applying facilitation skills. *See* Facilitation skills, four types

Assimilating and conceptualizing. *See* Learning processes; Learning activities

Beginning workshops, 51, 61, 63, 65, 69, 70, 97, 103, 104, 110, 166, 167, 168, 169
  introductions, 63, 69, 70, 73, 110-112, 166, 167, 168, 169
  overview, 63, 69, 70, 73, 112-114, 166, 167, 168

Common sense learners. *See* Learning styles, four types

Concluding workshops, 61, 63-64, 69, 70, 97, 103, 104, 116-117, 139, 166, 167, 168, 169
  feedback/evaluations, 117, 166, 167, 168
  follow-up, 117, 167, 168
  planning for the future, 116-117, 166, 167, 168
  reviewing content, 116, 166, 167, 168
  See also Evaluation

Consultant role, 47

Culture, impact on learning, 20, 36-37, 105

Design skills, xix, 11, 12, 14, 39-60, 61-74, 75, 157, 160
  alternate workshop structures, 63, 69-72, 162
  basic workshop structure, 69-70, 71, 73
  choosing a theme, 61, 62-63, 64, 73, 78, 80-81, 114, 161, 162, 163
  experimenting with, 163
  improving your, 157, 161-165
  personal preferences, 164
  rating your, 163
  sequencing learning activities, 61, 68-71, 161, 162, 163, 165
  using/implementing new, 164-165
  workshops of differing lengths, 61, 63, 71-72
  See also Beginning workshops; Concluding workshops; Design strategies; Learning activities, designing; Learning goals; Learning objectives; Preliminary information gathering

Design strategies 21, 64, 71-72, 161, 163
  measure and match, 21-22, 25-26, 29-30, 34-35, 64, 72, 161
  something for everyone, 21, 25, 27-29, 31-34, 64, 72, 161

Directing skills, 103, 110-117, 160
  experimenting/implementing, 166-167
  improving, 157, 165-169

maintaining a coherent message, 103,
104, 114-115, 166, 167, 168
rating your, 166, 168
See also Facilitation skills; Learning
environment; Pacing and timing
Director role, 65, 103, 108, 109, 114
Dunn and Dunn, 20, 26-30
See also Perceptual factors in learning;
Sociological factors in learning
Dynamic learners. See Learning styles, four
types

Engaging facilitation skills. See Facilitation
skills, four types
Evaluation, 73, 143-156, 162, 164
audience, 143, 144, 145
evaluator, 144, 145-146
process, 144
purpose, 143, 144
Evaluation plan, 143, 144, 152-155
analyzing information, 152, 154-155
collecting information, 152, 153-154
formulating questions and standards,
152-153
reporting information, 152, 155
selecting a research design, 152, 153
Evaluation strategies, 143, 144, 146-148, 149
combining strategies, 148, 149
formative vs. summative, 146-147, 149
150, 151
informal vs. formal, 146, 147-148, 149,
150, 151
quantitative vs. qualitative, 146, 147, 148,
149, 150, 151, 154
Evaluation variables, 143, 144, 148-152
accomplishment of learning objectives,
147, 149, 150-151
behavior change, 149, 151-152
satisfaction, 147, 149-150, 151
Experiential learning. See Kolb
Experiential learning cycle. See Kolb, cycle of
learning
Experiential processes. See Learning processes
Experimenting and practicing. See Learning
activities; Learning processes

Facilitation skills, xviii, xix, 6, 9, 11, 12, 13,
14, 16, 119-141, 160
assessing/rating, 120-122, 169-173
cofacilitation skills, 36, 126-127
experimenting with, 125-126, 171-173
improving your, 140-141, 157, 168-173
personal preferences, 124-125
Facilitation skills, four types, 14, 15, 16, 122,
125, 127, 169
applying, 14, 16, 122-123, 124, 125,
138-140, 169, 170, 173
engaging, 14, 15, 16, 122-123, 125,
127-131, 169, 170
informing, 14, 16, 122-123, 125, 131-134,
169, 171
involving, 14, 16, 122, 123, 124, 125, 127,
134-137, 169, 172
Facilitation skills examples, 127-140
answering questions, 121, 132, 171
asking for feedback, 73, 117, 121, 136,
172
asking for more information, 121, 129,
170
asking for reactions to an activity, 137, 172
assigning homework, 83, 121, 139, 173
bouncing questions back to the group, 8,
15, 54, 121, 130, 170, 172
brainstorming solutions, 73, 139-140, 173
challenging assumptions, 130, 170
clarifying, 132, 171
clarifying assumptions, 54, 110, 114,
131,166, 167, 168, 169, 171
clarifying expectations, 112, 113, 166,
167, 168
connecting participant ideas, 135, 172
directing traffic, 121
encouraging action, 121, 139, 173
encouraging brainstorming, 121, 130, 170
encouraging direct interaction, 121, 135,
172
encouraging goal setting, 121, 139, 173
encouraging interpersonal feedback, 137,
172
encouraging new behavior outside the
workshop, 73, 138, 173
encouraging new behavior within the
workshop, 82, 121, 134, 172
explaining, 121, 133-134, 171

exploring the future, 138, 173
focusing, 137, 172
generalizing from one environment to
    another, 138, 173
getting back on track, 137, 172
giving information, 121, 131, 171
identifying themes, 121, 132, 171
immediacy, 121, 136, 172
interpreting, 135, 172
modeling new behavior, 133, 171
paraphrasing, 15, 128, 170
pointing out opportunities for application,
    121, 138-139, 173
pointing out what was not mentioned,
    132, 171
previewing content or goals, 73, 115, 121,
    127, 170
probing, 129, 170
process observation, 136, 172
prompting participation, 121, 134, 172
punch lines, 114, 133, 171
questioning, 73, 95, 121, 129, 170
reflecting, 128, 170
reinforcing, 15, 129, 170
self-disclosure that increases motivation,
    121, 130-131, 170
self-disclosure that models application,
    121, 140, 173
self-disclosure that provides information,
    134, 171
setting ground rules/group norms, 110,
    113-114, 115, 121, 128, 166, 167,
    168, 170
summarizing, 115, 133, 171
surveying, 67, 121, 131, 171
Facilitator role, 1, 7-8, 11, 44, 103, 108, 120
    See also Facilitation skills
Feedback sources, 158
    attend other workshops, 160
    cofacilitator, 159, 164
    peer observation, 159
    questions to ask, 160
    requester, 159
    self-evaluation, 158-159, 164

Gender, impact on learning, 20, 35-36
Group dynamics, 43, 55

Imaginative learners. *See* Learning styles, four
    types
Improving your skills, 157-174
Informing facilitation skills. *See* Facilitation
    skills, four types
Involving facilitation skills. *See* Facilitation
    skills, four types
Integrated model of workshop development,
    xviii, xix, 1, 2, 14-16

Jung, C. G., 20, 30-35, 162
    extroversion-introversion, 20, 30-32, 71,
        84, 87, 93, 94, 96, 162, 164
    judging-perceiving, 31, 34
    sensing-intuition, 30, 31, 32-33, 86, 90,
        96, 98
    thinking-feeling, 30, 31, 33-34, 86, 95, 96,
        162

Kolb, D. A., 14, 22-26, 64
    cycle of learning, 9, 10, 13, 68-69, 70, 71,
        72, 116, 122, 162
    experiential learning, xviii, 1-2, 6, 7, 8-10,
        11, 12, 19-20, 22-26, 57, 68, 76, 103,
        104, 119, 120

Learners, four types. *See* Learning styles
Learning activities, xviii, xix, 6, 9, 11, 12, 13,
    25, 29, 31, 32, 33, 34, 63, 71, 75-101,
    106, 107, 120, 122, 124
    adapting for different types of learning,
        100, 161
    including different types of, 64, 161
Learning activities, designing, 25, 75-101,
    103, 161, 163
    assimilating and conceptualizing, 81-82,
        162
    experimenting and practicing, 82-83,
        162
    planning for application, 83, 162
    reflecting on experience, 78-81,
        162
Learning activity examples, 84-100
    action plans, 24, 32, 33, 73, 98
    art work, 28, 29, 33, 82, 95, 165

brainstorming, 15, 31, 32, 33, 73, 86
brainstorming solutions, 24, 99
card-sorting, 28, 29, 94
case studies, 32, 33, 69, 90
check-in/check-out, 97
dyadic sharing, 73, 80, 84-85
fishbowl discussions, 36, 91, 164
gallery exercises, 28, 29, 31, 32, 85-86
games, 31, 32, 57, 58, 87
goal setting, 32, 83, 98
group surveys, 33, 73, 88-89
guided fantasies, 32, 33, 34, 86-87
handouts, 28, 29, 31, 32, 33, 57, 58, 73,
    81, 82, 92, 117
homework, 24, 99
ice breakers, 15, 31, 84, 158
instruments, 31, 67, 81, 89
lectures/lecturettes, 28, 29, 33, 34, 73, 88,
    120, 123, 127
maps, 28, 29, 32, 33, 96
modeling role-plays, 69, 90, 100
motivation grabbers, 84
movement, 28, 29, 33, 81, 82, 90
music, 29, 33, 57, 58, 88
open discussions, 28, 29, 31, 34, 87, 91, 94
overheads, 28, 29, 57, 58, 81, 92
personal practice of skills learned in
    role-plays, 24, 97-98, 100
practice role-plays, 28, 29, 31, 32, 33, 34,
    67, 73, 92, 100
psychodrama, 28, 29, 31, 96-97, 164
questionnaires, 31, 32, 33, 51, 67, 81, 89
quizzes, 99
read-arounds, 28, 29, 31, 69, 91-92
scenarios, 73, 91, 95
simulations, 24, 31, 57, 58, 93, 134
small-group sharing, 84-85
sorting, 28, 29, 33, 51, 54, 90, 123
speak-outs, 31, 32, 100
stimulus role-plays, 85, 100
storytelling, 28, 29, 32, 87
structured discussions, 28, 29, 31, 67, 73,
    87, 91, 94-95
timelines, 29, 32, 33, 34, 96, 165
values clarification, 33, 34, 89, 90
videos, 57, 58, 59, 81, 92
worksheets, 24, 28, 29, 31, 32, 57, 58, 73,
    79, 81, 82, 93, 165

Learning activities, four types, 11, 15, 16,
    64-68, 75, 76
assimilating and conceptualizing, 16, 53,
    56-57, 58, 64, 65-67, 69, 70, 71, 73,
    77, 78, 81-82, 88-92, 100, 115, 123,
    163
experimenting and practicing, 16, 53, 57,
    58-59, 64, 65-68, 69, 70, 71, 73, 77,
    78, 82-83, 92-97, 100, 115, 124, 133,
    163
planning for application, 16, 53, 57, 59,
    64, 65-66, 68, 69, 70, 71, 73, 77, 78,
    83, 97-100, 115, 124, 164
reflecting on experience, 15, 16, 53, 56,
    58, 64-66, 69, 70, 71, 73, 77, 78-81,
    84, 100, 122, 163
See also Learning processes
Learning environment, xviii, 6, 7, 22, 24, 46,
    103, 104, 122, 128, 165, 167, 168
building trust and acceptance, 106,
    108-109, 165, 167, 168
encouraging/creating relationships,
    106-108, 165, 167, 168
multidirectional communication, 8, 106,
    108, 109, 165, 167, 168
physical environment, 46, 105-106, 107,
    165, 167, 168
providing encouragement, 106, 109-110,
    165, 167, 168
Learning goals, 39, 40, 43, 55, 62, 63, 73, 78,
    81, 82, 109, 110, 112-113, 115, 161,
    162, 163, 166, 167, 168
Learning modes, 9-10, 22, 68-69
abstract conceptualization, 9-10, 12, 22,
    23, 24, 67, 68-69
active experimentation, 9, 10, 12, 13, 20,
    22, 24, 67, 68-69
concrete experience, 9-10, 13, 22, 23, 24,
    68-69
reflective observation, 9-10, 12, 20, 22,
    23, 68-69
Learning needs. See Participant needs
Learning objectives, 39, 55-57, 62, 63, 71, 73,
    78, 81, 112-113, 116, 149, 150-151,
    161, 162, 163, 166, 167, 168
Learning processes, 9, 11, 115
assimilating and conceptualizing, 12, 13,
    14

experimenting and practicing, 12-13, 14
planning for application, 12, 13, 14, 116
reflecting on experience, 12, 13, 14, 15
Learning styles, xvii, xviii, xix, 6, 9-10, 11,
    12, 13, 14, 16, 19, 22 30, 36, 64, 76,
    122, 123
Learning styles, four types, 9-10, 11, 14, 16,
    65
  analytic learners, 9-10, 11, 14, 16, 22-23,
    24-25, 26, 64, 65, 67, 123
  common sense learners, 10, 11, 14, 16,
    22-24, 25, 64, 65, 67, 123, 124, 164
  dynamic learners, 10, 11, 14, 16, 22,
    23-24, 25, 64, 65, 68, 123, 124
  imaginative learners, 9, 11, 14, 15, 16, 22,
    23-24, 25, 64, 65, 122, 123
  See also Kolb; McCarthy
Learning Styles Inventory, 9, 11, 25-26
Learning theories, xix, 9-10, 11, 19-20, 22-35
  See also Dunn and Dunn; Jung; Kolb;
    McCarthy

McCarthy, B., 9-10, 14, 19-20, 22-26
Myers-Briggs Type Indicator, 30-31, 34-35,
    72, 89

Needs assessment, formal, 21, 22, 25, 39, 47,
    48-51, 62
Needs assessment, within workshops, 51-52
Needs prediction, 39, 48-49, 51

Pacing and timing, 45-46, 104, 115-116, 166,
    167, 168
Participant needs, 11, 13, 19, 22, 29, 47,
    48-52, 64, 122
  attitude, 54
  knowledge, 53
  motivation, 54-55
  See also Learning styles; Needs
    assessment
Perceptual factors in learning, 26, 162
  auditory, 20, 27, 28-30, 87, 88, 91, 94,
    162, 164
  kinesthetic, 20, 27, 28-30, 90, 93, 96, 162,
    164

tactile, 20, 27, 28-30, 93, 94, 95, 162, 164
  visual, 20, 27, 28-30, 85, 92, 95, 96, 162
  See also Dunn and Dunn
Personality factors in learning. *See* Jung
Planning for application. *See* Learning
  activities; Learning processes
Preliminary information gathering, 39, 41-47,
    161, 162, 163
Preparation time and effort, 40-41, 45
Productivity Environmental Preference
  Survey, 29 30
Reflecting on experience. *See* Learning
  activities; Learning processes
Requester/initiator needs, 41, 42-43, 49,
    52-53, 159
  See also Stakeholders
Resources, additional:
  types of, 57
  using to promote experiential learning, 39,
    57-59

Sociological factors in learning, 26, 27-28, 29,
    30, 105
  See also Dunn and Dunn
Stakeholders, 43, 52, 145, 152

Teaching-learning activities. *See* Learning
  activities

Understanding workshop participants, xviii,
    11-12

Wizard of Oz, xvii-xviii, 24-25
Workshop activities. *See* Learning activities
Workshop agreement, 39, 47-48, 49
Workshop content, 41, 42, 43, 45
Workshop definitions, 1, 2-3, 6-7, 45
Workshop design skills. *See* Design skills
Workshop design strategies. *See* Design
  strategies
Workshop development, 2, 10-15
Workshop development tasks, 10-12
Workshop emphases, 1, 2
  increasing knowledge, 4-5, 63

interaction among emphases, 4-5
personal awareness/self-improvement,
    4-5, 63
problem solving, 3, 4, 5, 63
skill building, 3, 4, 5, 63, 115
systemic change, 4-5, 63
Workshop environment. *See* Learning
    environment
Workshop evaluations. *See* Evaluation

Workshop facilitation. *See* Facilitation skills;
    Facilitator role
Workshop purpose, 41, 45
    See also Workshop emphases
Workshop title, 42, 44-45
Workshop topic, 40, 41, 42, 44, 75, 76, 78, 80,
    81, 82, 83, 84, 85, 87, 88, 90, 92, 96,
    112, 134, 137

About the Authors

Jeff E. Brooks-Harris is a psychologist at the Counseling and Student Development Center at the University of Hawai'i at Manoa where he coordinates outreach activities for the center. He received his PhD in Counseling Psychology from The Ohio State University in 1990. He has extensive workshop design and facilitation experience, having presented hundreds of workshops on dozens of different topics. Most of this workshop experience has been on the four university campuses where he has worked. He has coordinated the outreach activities for two university counseling centers and has trained professionals, interns, and graduate students on workshop design and facilitation. He recently has begun to coordinate a website called Workshop Central (http://www2.hawaii.edu/~jharris/workshophome.html) that allows university counseling center professionals to share workshop resources. His long-time interest in workshop design and experience in training others as facilitators naturally has led to his interest in developing the present book. Other areas of professional interest include psychotherapy integration, emotions, clinical training and supervision, multicultural issues, and gender. He is the coauthor of an instructor's manual titled *Teaching Men's Lives* (Messina-Yauchzy, Brooks-Harris, & Gertner, 1998).

Susan R. Stock-Ward is a psychologist at the Counseling, Testing, and Career Center at the University of Akron where she coordinates outreach and staff development activities. She received her PhD in Counseling Psychology from Iowa State University in 1995. She has several years of workshop design and facilitation experience dating back to an undergraduate position as a living/learning center program advisor at the University of Illinois. Most of her workshop experience has been on the five university campuses where she has worked. This long-standing interest and involvement in workshops has led her to train many different groups of students and professionals in these skills, as well as to write this book. She has always found it ironic that workshop facilitation is a skill required in many professions, yet little training exists. She hopes that this book helps remedy that deficit. Other areas of professional interest include clinical training and supervision, multicultural issues, career development, and body image and disordered eating. This is her first book.